"Thank you Michael Todd for the gift of *Unburdened*. It gives men permission and opportunity to crack open the vault and be honest about their sexual integrity. I wish I could turn back time and accept this book's invitation to be honest and transparent with my own sexual integrity struggles. This book is a must-read and re-read for every Christian leader. For more than five years, MT's insight, care and leadership have been crucial in my own recovery from sexual integrity failures as a ministry leader. As I read *Unburdened*, I felt as if I were face-to-face with MT, talking about this crucial topic that most men desperately avoid."

Steve Fee, songwriter, worship leader, music producer

"Finding sexual integrity for pastors and church leaders is one of the most significant challenges of our age. Despite this desperate need for recovery, too many Christian leaders feel isolated and alone and suffer in quiet despair and shame. Michael Todd Wilson clearly lays out a thorough plan of healing and recovery in the pages of this book that will give you hope for the future. Thank you, Michael Todd, for being a pastor to our pastors and church leaders!"

Gary D. Campbell, CFA, president, PCA Retirement & Benefits, Inc.

"Michael Todd Wilson's *Unburdened* is spot-on. This book will be an invaluable tool as I minister to men in our congregation and men serving as missionaries all over the world. The struggle with sexual integrity is not confined to western culture and its trappings. Men serving in some of the most remote places in the world have the same struggles. This book will save ministries!"

Ricky Wheeler, global ministries, Johnson Ferry Baptist Church

"For many years I have worked alongside Michael Todd Wilson as a trusted colleague—coauthoring a book, sharing conference platforms and witnessing his effectiveness in working with Christian men in sexual integrity recovery. I am excited that he has distilled the wisdom of many years of professional work into his book *Unburdened*. It contains practical steps for guiding men into a God-empowered sexual integrity with many helpful stories and examples. I highly recommend this book, not only for those struggling through sexual brokenness, but for all men in Christian leadership as we work together to achieve the sexual integrity we so desire."

Doug Rosenau, psychologist, cofounder, Sexual Wholeness, Inc.

"What an amazing book! You open it expecting to find some practical advice on dealing with sexual temptation as a Christian leader (and you do!). But what you soon realize is that Michael Todd Wilson has such a fantastic grasp on the struggles of Christian leaders in general, you end up being ministered to in areas you never expected. Will this book help with sexual struggles? Undoubtedly. But expect it to do more. Expect it to help you become a better follower of Jesus and a better leader. Required reading for every seminarian. Highly recommended!"

Bruce Lowe, assistant professor of New Testament, Reformed Theological Seminary

UNBURDENED

THE CHRISTIAN LEADER'S
PATH TO SEXUAL INTEGRITY

∎∎✝∎∎

MICHAEL TODD WILSON

≈
IVP Books

An imprint of InterVarsity Press
Downers Grove, Illinois

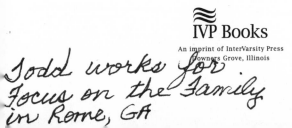
Todd works for
Focus on the Family
in Rome, GA

InterVarsity Press
P.O. Box 1400, Downers Grove, IL 60515-1426
ivpress.com
email@ivpress.com

InterVarsity Press® is the book-publishing division of InterVarsity Christian Fellowship/USA®, a
movement of students and faculty active on campus at hundreds of universities, colleges and schools
of nursing in the United States of America, and a member movement of the International Fellowship
of Evangelical Students. For information about local and regional activities, visit intervarsity.org.

While any stories in this book are true, some names and identifying information may have been
changed to protect the privacy of individuals.

Cover design: Cindy Kiple
Interior design: Beth McGill
Images: © carloscastilla/iStockphoto

ISBN 978-0-8308-4432-6 (print)
ISBN 978-0-8308-9878-7 (digital)

Printed in the United States of America ∞

Library of Congress Cataloging-in-Publication Data
Wilson, Michael Todd.
  Unburdened : the Christian leader's path to sexual integrity / Michael Todd Wilson.
    pages cm
  Includes bibliographical references.
  ISBN 978-0-8308-4432-6 (pbk. : alk. paper)
  1. Christian leadership. 2. Christian men—Sexual behavior. I. Title.
BV652.1.W5148 2015
241'.4--dc23
                                                                    2015018836

P   20 19 18 17 16 15 14 13 12 11 10 9 8 7 6 5 4 3 2 1
Y   32 31 30 29 28 27 26 25 24 23 22 21 20 19 18 17 16 15

This book is dedicated to men who serve

the Lord in various capacities as Christian leaders.

Whether as pastors, church staffers, nonprofit directors,

counselors, speakers, missionaries, Christian businessmen, elders,

lay leaders, husbands or fathers, you are on the front lines

day in and day out. As men, so many areas of our lives

rise and fall with the quality of our sexual integrity.

What follows is for any man with enough

humility to open it for the purpose

of improving his own

integrity walk.

CONTENTS

ACKNOWLEDGMENTS

■■✝■■

"Can you provide me with an updated email address for someone?"

I was simply wanting to contact someone at InterVarsity Press who'd worked on my previous book, *Preventing Ministry Failure*. His email address changed, a detail I noticed when a weekly newsletter I send bounced back to me. I was simply trying to update my email list.

"If you have an idea for a book, let us know. We'd love to talk to you about it," her email replied.

"I wasn't emailling about a book proposal, but I guess I've always got a few ideas in my head," I responded.

And so this book began to take shape. More intentional on God's part than my own, I'd say. But honestly, that's probably the way it needed to be. Without that prompt, I'm not sure I would have written it.

Credit is due to a number of sources beyond myself. First, I'm grateful for the hundreds of Christian leaders I've walked alongside whose stories include a broken sexual road. While none of their stories are directly told in "Our Fellow Journeymen" (chapter two), they are the chapter's source of inspiration. Without my experiences alongside them on their respective recovery journeys, this book simply would not be. *Their lessons through failure have now become lessons for proactive health and thriving for the rest of us.*

Second, thank you to the dozens of men (and a few significant women too) who've looked at various versions of this manuscript including counseling colleagues, seminary professors, Christian ministry leaders and a few clients and buddies. Thanks for your critical feedback and significant encouragement along the way.

Third, thanks to Helen Lee and the editorial team at InterVarsity Press. Even though this is my third published book, I never cease to be amazed at how much better the final product is than the early manuscripts. The editorial team is the "secret sauce" of any good writing project. This time around has been no exception.

Fourth, a ton of credit goes to my wife, Tanya. Many a night (and a few key weekends) she sacrificed tirelessly, taking care of our two preschoolers to make this project possible. While many have compared writing a book with pregnancy and childbirth, her labor in this process was, in many ways, greater than my own.

Finally, as I've already mentioned, this book originated with and terminates in God and his purposes. My heart is to see this book help men in all forms of Christian leadership avoid heartache and loss due to moral failure. The best way for the rest of us to do that is to learn from those who've experienced it firsthand and to intentionally practice principles that will either get us back on the road to integrity or help us avoid the detours in the first place.

I ask for grace for any errors you'll likely encounter in this book. But more than a desire to be a grace recipient, I want to be a *grace conduit*. It's my earnest desire to help you, the Christian leader, experience God's grace along the path to sexual integrity.

Yes, there *is* absolute truth. We both wholeheartedly agree to that. But where we fall short (and we all do to some degree), there is also *redemption*—even for the Christian leader.

May we walk by grace alone, and only for his glory.

1

WELCOME TO THE PATH

*The author who benefits you most is not the one who tells you
something you did not know before, but the one who gives
expression to the truth that has been dumbly
struggling in you for utterance.*

OSWALD CHAMBERS,
MY UTMOST FOR HIS HIGHEST (DECEMBER 15)

■■✝■■

Tom and Jonathan have been racquetball buddies for years. Every
Tuesday, they get together at the gym for a competitive, yet friendly
rematch.

"Did you hear about Pastor Phillip's affair?" Jonathan said in disbelief.
"I can't believe it's true. I'd never have guessed it would happen to him.
Lots of people at his church are really angry right now. Might even
cause a split. I just don't understand what causes somebody to take that
kind of risk and lose everything that matters to them. Do you?"

Tom felt his muscles tense and a sinking feeling in the pit of his
stomach. His mind raced with thoughts for changing the subject or
finding some socially acceptable response. Though he'd never engaged in an affair, Tom regularly battled lustful thoughts about
women and sometimes became preoccupied with searching the

Internet for R-rated movies with sex scenes, though he never really understood why.

Jonathan's tone caused Tom to feel as if he were being interrogated.

"No idea," Tom replied, trying to hide his emotional defensiveness. "I have no idea."

A TALE OF TWO QUESTIONS

"Do you struggle with sexual integrity?" seems like a straightforward enough question.

But now consider another question: "*How* do you struggle with sexual integrity?"

The two sentences only differ by one word. Yet the difference between them represents a significant shift I'd like to see among Christian leadership.

The first question begs us to not tell the truth or, at least, to tell only part of the truth. The second question not only makes the assumption that we struggle in some way, but it also signals it's okay to talk about it.

The first question tends to trigger our fear-driven fight-or-flight response. Confronted with only two options for answering, the knee-jerk response of many would be, "No, not really."

But the second question feels safer and invites conversation beyond a simple yes or no answer, causing a shift away from defensiveness toward a freedom to engage in honest dialogue.

These two questions represent the difference between shame and grace, law and love.

AN HONEST VIEW OF THE PATH

Among clergy, a 2009 study conducted by Texas Tech University of 460 male ministers revealed over 20 percent accessed pornography at least twice monthly.[1] Older statistics on Christian clergy showed anywhere from 35 to 50 percent of ministers consider pornography a personal struggle, whether currently or in the past.[2]

As Christian leaders, these stats don't really tell us anything we don't already know. Porn is a significant issue for both Christian men and Christian leaders alike. And that's just about pornography. This says nothing about our sexual integrity struggles with prostitution on business trips, strip clubs, affairs, masturbation, unbridled fantasy and checking out the sexy jogger in the rearview mirror.

At some level, sexual integrity is challenging for all of us. Some experience good success; some don't. But the challenge to that integrity is *everywhere*.

This is true for Christian leaders across the spectrum. Anyone with a leadership role in the lives of other believers—pastors and clergy in traditional settings, denominational leaders, Christian nonprofit leaders, Christian small business owners, Christian counselors, elders, deacons and church small-group leaders—we all have feet of clay. *None* of us are somehow beyond the struggles of any other men in our sex-saturated culture.

AN UNCONVENTIONAL APPROACH

This book isn't primarily about how to stop looking at porn or any other unhealthy or compulsive sexual behavior. Unlike a decade or two ago, it's no longer hard to find good Christian books about how to combat pornography and sexual addiction. Many of the titles I've used in my professional coaching with men and Christian leaders in sexual integrity recovery can be found in appendix C.

This is also not a book about blaming others for our poor sexual choices. And it's most certainly not about stirring up more shame. As Christian leaders, we need safe places for honest and profitable dialogue about sexual integrity.

No, this book isn't so much about equipping as it is about *giving permission.* Permission to work through our fear and internal resistance so we can simply take one single step in the direction of greater sexual integrity. Each of us pays a price when we're unable—both individually and collectively as Christian leaders—to take ownership (privately and publicly) of our common struggle to maintain sexual integrity.

Notice, I didn't say our common struggle with engaging sexual sin. Engaging sexual sin is optional; contending for sexual integrity isn't.

When we don't feel permission to be honest about our common struggle to maintain sexual integrity, we're more likely to fall morally and lose what really matters: loss of ministry, marriage and family; loss of money; lost enjoyment in ministry; isolation from friends, colleagues and mentors. Not to mention an increased distraction away from our ultimate goal of impacting the kingdom—to the point of potentially becoming irrelevant in ministry.

If we can't own our common struggle to maintain sexual integrity as Christian leaders, the consequences can find us seemingly without warning. Maybe some of us have been so successful playing Russian roulette that we forget one of the chambers is loaded. Even hearing about someone like Pastor Phillip—which happens more frequently than we care to admit—doesn't always get our attention.

PERSONAL APPLICATION OF THE TRUTH

It doesn't matter who we are or how high up we are in Christian leadership. This message applies to all of us. Our purpose in the kingdom will only be accomplished to the extent we don't allow spiritual disease into our life that siphons off our strength.

Samson was a powerful man of God, but he had a huge problem that bled out his strength. God accomplished much through King David, a man after God's own heart. But his sexual sins were passed down to his kids and grandkids, causing untold pain for generations.

I realize this is a sensitive subject. We're afraid (and rightly so) with what the consequences might be if we start to honestly deal with it, publicly or privately. But deep down we all know that we *have* to deal with it if we're going to fulfill God's ultimate purpose in our lives. To deal with it will challenge our growth in our own understanding of God's sufficiency, a message we all too easily preach to others. Our personal application of this message has the power to free up a more passionate and authentic message of hope for others—because it will have been God's message of hope applied to our own lives *first*.

We need fearless courage to apply this message to ourselves before seeking to apply it to the men we lead. It doesn't matter whether we're completely enslaved to sexual addiction, or whether we periodically struggle with pornography or glance at women in church for a few seconds too long. When our lives are humbly transformed, God empowers us with a grace to not only resist evil but to encourage and empower other men to do likewise. Other men won't just be hearing our words; they'll be seeing our lives in transformation.

That's the kind of Christian leadership every man can't help but follow.

If those we lead hear us speaking like a broken man—with humility because of our own journey in progress—our example will be more compelling than all the words we could string together over an entire lifetime of ministry. I'm not necessarily saying we have to tell our story publicly, although God may certainly convict us to do so at some point along the way. Even if we never share the details publicly, one of the most compelling things that influence other men is a Christian leader's testimony about his own imperfection and his honest sharing of God's santifying work in his own life.

Honestly, our pride is the biggest roadblock standing between our staying stuck and the difficult but incredible journey of redemption. It can totally transform our ministry effectiveness. I'm not talking about improving our ability to build a big organization or ministry following. We can do that while still living in unchecked sexual sin. Examples of this are, unfortunately, plentiful. I'm not talking about building a narcissistic monument to our own great leadership. I'm talking about building a lasting legacy in the lives of others, whether that impact numbers in the dozens or millions.

Real transformation is deeper than it is wide. And deep change, sustained over time in the life of one person, was a primary task Jesus left for us to steward. It's called making disciples.

A GLIMPSE AHEAD

Over the past ten years, I've personally walked with hundreds of men down the path of sexual integrity recovery. Many of these men served in various roles of Christian leadership. Some lost ministry and family, others didn't. Some were afraid to take the steps necessary and veered off the path. I fear what happened to them.

But those who kept placing one foot in front of the other eventually saw fruit from their investment. Many who stayed in ministry or eventually returned to it report having a stronger ministry impact, especially in seeing others transformed at deeper levels than before. They report increased opportunities for influence, though this sometimes resulted in doing ministry in a new or different capacity. Those whose marriages survived (and more did than didn't) report both increased respect from and increased relational intimacy with their spouse. And regardless of the survival of their marriage or ministry, nearly all discovered increased support through closer relationships with other men (including other Christian leaders) and with God.

While the consequences of not walking this path can strike suddenly and without warning, the benefits emerge slowly with time and persistence. This is another reason why not every Christian leader is eager to take the journey. It's like a medical treatment that has early side effects but whose eventual benefits aren't experienced until a prolonged course of treatment.

Maybe we feel overwhelmed in knowing how to take the first step. Maybe we're simply scared to death of it. Or maybe we've taken steps to move away from past sin and just don't know what our next growth step might be.

Welcome to the path.

In my professional work, many began this journey involuntarily because something happened: a spouse discovered their Internet searches, they were caught in their double life by another employee at work or something of that nature. If we met them somewhere on the path, they'd say, "Don't wait until the decision's made for you. Do something now, so *you* get to choose the way and timing of your growth."

They learned the hard way. But we can learn from their failure without the need to suffer nearly as many consequences. Yes, there are certainly consequences to voluntarily sharing our struggle with a Christian counselor, mentor, ministry colleague or spouse. But being caught in our struggle rather than voluntarily sharing it results in greater mistrust and disillusionment on the part of others. This is especially true for a spouse. As I often tell my clients, disclosure almost always turns out better than discovery. The consequences are either the same or better—not worse.

At the end of the day, I'm not really hung up on whether we accept a label such as *sex addict* or *sexually compulsive* or *sexual sinner*. I don't care whether we accept a label at all. My greatest concern is that whatever we do, we accept responsibility for admitting where we are and for how far we've strayed from our Father's heart. Like many of the perils in *Pilgrim's Progress*, there are lots of ways to subtly veer from the King's Highway onto some alternate path leading to danger and destruction.

But no matter how far off course we find ourselves, the correction for each of us is the same: admitting where we are, turning back toward the Father and taking one step toward home.

Then another one. Then another. All the way home.

The farther out we've traveled, the longer it may take us to travel home. That's okay. We'll still get home along the same pathway that took us toward the pigsty in the first place.

There's no shame here. Only a decision to either continue the same old dusty, lonely path or turn around and face the risks and rewards of rebuilding the life we left back home.

A COUNTERCULTURAL PATH

I fully realize the suggestions I'm making here could be interpreted by some within the Christian leadership community as dangerous. Some will say the grace offered here is risky, especially when it's being applied to Christian leaders.

But if grace applies to anyone in the church, it must also apply to the Christian leader—regardless of whether he tells anyone else his secret struggles. While not everyone needs public disclosure, *all* of us need at least one or two people who know our whole story and can walk alongside us in the road ahead. Yes, in a perfect world, I would want a Christian leader who's seriously struggling in this area to take a sabbatical from his ministry or work responsibilities to more fully address these issues. But I understand the realities of men and I understand the realities of men in ministry. I know the consequences that potentially await a Christian leader who raises a public red flag in this arena. Sometimes, he gets supportive sympathy. Other times, he locks eyes with an angry bull.

One fifty-something executive pastor was fired and now works in secular employment. An associate minister was let go immediately after looking at pornography on the church's computer. One music minister was terminated after an emotional affair, yet was eventually restored a few years later to leading worship in a different church as the result of the intentional work of a restoration committee. Another worship pastor transitioned to parachurch ministry under similar circumstances.

Three of these men kept and eventually strengthened their marriages through all of the turbulence; one divorced.

While every man's circumstance is unique, I personally think the risk of taking the countercultural path is worth it in the long run. Even for the one who divorced, God has done an amazing work of restoration in other areas of his ministry and personal life. I've seen God rebuild leaders and ministries from the ground up, stronger than they were before. Even if you're not completely convinced of my perspective, just know that, a willingness to take *any* step is a step in a helpful direction, with or without public disclosure. I know that with each successive step, there's a greater likelihood you'll keep on walking.

I'm not going to play the role of the Holy Spirit here. That's his job. Just consider me another prodigal brother who's gently nudging you back toward our dear Father.

After all, we've all got a story to tell.

A PERSONAL NOTE

My wife and I are parents of two preschoolers, one of whom is autistic, so we know a thing or two about challenging life circumstances. However, throughout the early stage of writing this manuscript we faced a number of unusual challenges from a variety of sources. While we deal with our share of medical issues as a family, this has been at least three standard deviations beyond the norm. I believe there was something more sinister at play in all this.

Our enemy doesn't want you to take seriously the possibility of sexual integrity beyond the path you're already walking. If you do, you'll experience greater freedom, increased clarity in your ability to hear the Lord and sense his presence, heightened focus in your ability to carry out your leadership calling, and more faithfulness as a husband and father. Perhaps most importantly, if you seriously pursue this path, your life will become an unburdened vessel that's fully surrendered to what the Lord wants to accomplish through you in our world.

That's a serious threat to the kingdom of darkness.

Take encouragement from our stories and from the lessons we've learned. You, your family and your ministry will benefit. Not only that, you can become a catalyst for changing the culture among Christian leaders in making openness around these issues more acceptable.

There's not a one of us who doesn't face real challenges to our personal sexual integrity. Can we for once be honest about that? The more honest we can be with each other, the healthier we'll become as Christian leaders and as a church. The more surrendered we are to the Lord on these matters, the more effective we'll be as servants of the Living God.

It's worth the journey.

2

OUR FELLOW JOURNEYMEN

Christian: *"Tell me about the things you experienced as you traveled. I know you met with some things. If not, it should be written up as a miracle."*

Faithful: *"I escaped the Slough that I perceive you fell into, and made it to the gate without that danger. However, I met one whose name was Wanton and she almost caused me harm."*

JOHN BUNYAN, *PILGRIM'S PROGRESS*

My dear friends, if you know people who have wandered off from God's truth, don't write them off. Go after them. Get them back and you will have rescued precious lives from destruction and prevented an epidemic of wandering away from God.

JAMES 5:20 *THE MESSAGE*

Daniel was a Christian speaker well-respected in his area of expertise. Before becoming a Christian, Daniel was an alcoholic. He came to Christ in his twenties, at which time God did a radical transformation in his life. With the help of a strong AA community, Daniel got into solid recovery—at least from the alcohol.

Daniel never really liked traveling alone and being away from his wife, with whom he had a fairly good relationship. His insecurities were fed by the appreciation and praise from those to whom he ministered on the road, men and women alike. Yet with women, Daniel's emotional boundaries were more fuzzy. He never realized just how many of his emotional desires were stroked in these interactions. Although he actually longed for such emotional validation from his bride back home, his high-energy style of networking made him vulnerable to flirting with women in the hotel bars where he traveled. These challenges were in addition to the occasional viewing of sexually oriented content on the TV in his hotel room.

Daniel got on the path after his wife discovered a woman's email scrawled on a napkin in his suit pocket.

■ ■ ■

Matt was a nonprofit director whose relational style was introverted and somewhat timid. Over the years, he learned to use these personality traits to his advantage, as others tended to trust him more readily because of his easygoing nature. But it also led to lifelong struggles with passivity.

This passivity fed into his preoccupation with online pornography, which had increased steadily with time. Because he was such a likable and unassuming guy, no one thought to question the nondescript packaging that began to be delivered to his desk periodically, which contained mail-order porn.

Matt joined the journey after someone unsuspectingly opened one of his special deliveries.

■ ■ ■

James was a winsome rural pastor who consistently gave artfully crafted sermons and was loved by his congregation. Yet, parts of his personal life were completely hidden from everyone, including his wife. He worked long hours, or so it appeared. Anytime James was away from the church, people assumed he was visiting members who were in the hospital, or that he was running a personal errand. But beneath his perfectionistic pastoral exterior was a secret life consumed with pursuing one-night stands found from hours trolling a popular dating website.

James wouldn't have joined the path on his own. It took the shock of an arrest—followed by months of denial and minimization—to finally convince him to join his fellow journeymen.

■ ■ ■

Ben was a never-married, up-and-coming Christian leader with a great mentor and a big heart for ministry. He devoured every book he could find on leadership and ministry growth. With dreams of having high impact in ministry came the stress and anxiety of the pressure to perform. Under the gun to make his mentor proud, pornography was his means for escape. Sometimes, it served as a distraction for putting off work he didn't want to deal with that day. At other times, he subconsciously reached for it as a reward at the end of a fourteen-hour day of successful ministry.

Underlying his interest in porn was his ultimate desire to have a real relationship with a godly woman. In addition to the shame of being an unmarried single in his thirties, he experienced further shame in that the content of his pornography often included S & M bondage fantasies. This added to his fears that he would never find a Christian woman who could love and accept him. Ben had to push down an overwhelming sense of shame each time his mentor gave him opportunity to teach.

Ben voluntarily reached out to the path after an online search to find someone who could help make sense of his preoccupying fantasies.

■ ■ ■

Tim was a worship leader who, like most men, enjoyed superficial friendships with many. He enjoyed a great relationship with his wife in every area—other than sexually. When it came to sex, his shame sometimes prevented him from engaging her in a meaningful way. For Tim, he struggled to not allow his internal impulses toward men to define him sexually. This core belief had been around for so long, he found it difficult to recognize the satanic lie around which his core belief existed. Tim struggled with the internal label *gay*, though he was still very much sexually attracted to both men and women—including his wife, Jillian. If he were honest, his impulses toward men at times felt more defining than the cross of his Savior.

Tim had never acted on his impulses other than masturbation to fantasies in his head, which unfortunately were somewhat frequent. Of course, engaging those fantasies significantly reduced his frequency of sexual initiative toward his wife, which had resulted in significant dissatisfaction for both of them over the years.

Tim finally joined up after becoming worn out from his wife's begging him to get help for his lack of sexual pursuit in the bedroom. She knew about his past struggle with same-sex attractions, but she assumed it was more a thing of the past. She had no idea how burdensome these impulses still were for Tim. That is, until now.

DIFFERENT MEN, SAME STORY

The men above are actually composite characters, formed from my professional experiences with dozens of clients. You'll be meeting each of these characters again later as we follow their journey toward greater sexual integrity.

By God's grace and through no merit of my own, I've not paid nearly the consequences others have in dealing with these issues. But don't confuse that with a lack of understanding. I, too, struggled to get on the path. My parents were by no means perfect, but they did many things right as people of faith. I didn't grow up with cable, nor did I have access to pornographic magazines from an early age. The most pornographic content in our home was the lingerie section of the JCPenney's catalog. Yet, along with the fertility of my own fantasy, this was enough to preoccupy my newly sexually charged, tween-age brain.

Looking back, I can now see that these fantasies, along with my accidental discovery of masturbation, filled the void left by my general lack of popularity, insecurity, geekiness, slender build, loneliness as an only child and general feeling that I was responsible for the reputation of the family name as its sole offspring. I learned early on that what I lacked through natural intelligence I could make up for with sheer elbow grease.

But when the pressure of this became too great, or when it didn't work as well as I'd hoped and yielded its share of disappointments, I turned elsewhere for comfort.

I don't remember how often masturbation occurred in my adolescence, but I seriously doubt it occurred more often than for most boys. It's been said that 99 percent of American boys masturbate and that the other 1 percent are lying. Maybe that's an exaggeration, but the point is still well taken. All of us deal with sexual tension. Most of us, if not all, learned to express that tension in various broken ways littered throughout our childhood, adolescence and early adulthood.

My first actual exposure to pornography didn't happen until the summer between my junior and senior year in college. I received an internship with an insurance company out of town, and the company provided an executive suite to live in for the summer.

Unbeknownst to me, the apartment had cable and one of the channels free for the watching showed late-night adult movies.

Many a night I stayed up late, allowing my curiosity to take in what most boys had previously experienced or had at least been exposed to in their younger years. Subconsciously, I probably justified it that way, given I'd never experimented with drugs, gotten into legal trouble and was generally a teacher's pet at school.

This cable box freebie seemed innocent enough. After all, it became my de facto sex education, picking up where James Dobson's *Preparing for Adolescence* necessarily left off. Little did I know I was opening up a Pandora's box, one that most Christian boys longing to become men wished they'd never opened.

I rarely lived outside of my "nice Christian guy" box, if for nothing else than fear that someone else would see and judge me. At the same time, my true moral compass didn't really want to engage in such sexual activity. I surrendered my life to Christ at thirteen during a Fellowship of Christian Athletes week-long summer camp in Black Mountain, North Carolina, and my surrender to Christ was real.

But so was the pull of lust and fantasy.

I had limited access to pornography until the advent of the Internet. At that point, everything changed. Suddenly, all the things outside my "nice Christian guy" reach became easily available and seemingly anonymous. From my twenties and into my early thirties, there was a constant pull toward and push away from Internet pornography.

Then in my early thirties, something shifted. I began to experience a greater internal desire for becoming a man of integrity. I can't tell you exactly how this happened, although there were a few contributing factors. It was early in my career as a counselor when my mentor encouraged me to specialize. I had a desire for helping Christian men deal with pornography, both for the benefit of the church at large as well as for myself. At the same time, I was going through Robert Lewis's original *Men's Fraternity*[1] and became serious about my transition from insecure to mature Christian masculinity. As a single thirty-something, I'd also finally gotten in touch with the longing to pursue a wife. I'd also recently connected into a strong church community with a number of Christian men who invited me to engage life alongside them.

These came together to create an environment that offered safety, confidence and (perhaps most importantly) permission within safe relationships to finally take the first meaningful step away from pornography and toward a more mature Christian walk.

NOT THE BEGINNING, BUT CERTAINLY NOT THE END

Now, I won't tell you this was the end of the story. It wasn't. But it *was* the beginning, and I haven't turned back. I won't. The path from that day to today hasn't been linear, but rather a jagged and gradually inclining slope of "straining toward what is ahead" (Phil 3:13 NIV).

Sometimes I still make poor choices with what my eyes see, more often in my environment than on the Internet. My brain still overinterprets sexual stimuli. But there's a difference in my response today from years ago. When I act on my impulses rather than my Christian values, I try to take ownership of it as quickly as possible. I admit it to myself, to God and one other person, in the tradition of the Twelve Steps. If it's the kind of fantasy that only preoccupies my thinking, I share it with God and one of a few Christian men in my life. If it also includes accessing any sort of porn, I also tell my wife.

The last thing I want is to let my shame keep me in darkness, isolated by fear far from my wife and my closest male relationships. Satan kept me duped far too long, and I don't want to go back to that life. I want to live in the light, and keeping this in mind has been my best source of freedom.

For me, this is practical sanctification. I'm not perfect, but I'm way more perfected than I've ever been in my sexual integrity experience. With each temptation, through relative success or failure, God continues to perfect me. And I expect to continue being perfected until the day I see my Coach face to face at the finish line.

REDEEMER AT WORK

In each of these stories—mine included—God is actively at work redeeming the mess. Some of us remain in ministry, some not. We are being sanctified as a result of applying these simple principles. More than that, each of us is being slowly transformed by the great grace of the gospel—a grace that applies to Christian leaders just as it does to the worst of sinners (Lk 18:9-14).

For the men represented here, our lives are by no means perfect. Nor do I mean to imply we haven't paid a price—in some cases a heavy price—for being on this path. But each one would tell you it's been worth it.

For those who've lost marriages, lost ministries or incurred significant financial debt as a result of poor choices, they likely wouldn't have said the journey was worth it at the initial point of impact of their consequences. I suppose God knew their respective crises were necessary to get their attention. As C. S. Lewis said, "But pain insists upon being attended to. God whispers to us in our pleasures, speaks in our conscience, but shouts in our pains. It is his megaphone to rouse a deaf world."[2] Sometimes, God doesn't hesitate to use tough circumstances to break through our denial and to help us see things as he sees them.

For many of my clients, their external crises were great. For others like me, they were relatively small. Yet for all of us, the internal pain spoke loud and clear and was used by God to accomplish his purpose in getting us on this path.

Some may ask what distinguishes those who eventually embrace the path from those who don't. From God's view, it's simply a practical manifestation of his grace towards us. But on a human plane, there were a few key realizations in retrospect that had significant impact.

Surrender. In our brokenness, we thought God was withholding sexual fulfillment from us. We believed Satan's lies that he was the only one who cared about our sexual thirst. In walking with a few others who'd been down the path ahead of us, we came to realize God for who he is, a loving dad who wants nothing more than for us to grow up into his image. Now, we're learning to surrender the lies we once believed about ourselves and our sexuality. We've slowly redirected our anger away from God, ourselves and those who may have forced our recovery and turned it back toward our real enemy.

Sanctification. We are laying down our old ways of coping. Where we once relied on hiding behind masks (like perfectionism and people pleasing), we understand the path in front of us doesn't have to be perfect because we're trusting in the one who's already finished the journey with perfection. In humility, we understand the path can't be traveled all at once, but rather only one choice at a time. And that's ok. There's great freedom in being responsible only for the next step, knowing that each one results in even more freedom and redemption than the one before. We've also realized we don't have to walk the path alone. Jesus our Rescuer, the Holy Spirit our Comforter and a band of a few close Christian brothers actually *want* to walk with us every step of the way. This is a big change from the isolation we once experienced as being "just the way it is" in Christian leadership.

Celebration. Yes, we do have the guarantee (what the Bible calls *hope*) that we'll ultimately reach the end of the race, where our Coach will embrace us with a bear hug and a "Welcome home, Son!" at the finish line. But we've also learned to see and celebrate small victories along the way. The more we take risks to put into practice the principles presented here—and do them while staying intimately connected with our closest relationships—the more we see the practical fruit of redemption at work. We're not perfect, but redemption is at work in ways that demonstrate we're *being perfected* with each next step.

These simple truths weave together the fabric of our narrative. Again, there are lots of books out there about how to avoid pornography, make amends, address underlying emotional wounds from childhood and so on. I don't sense the need to reinvent the wheel on these.

Honestly, my passion for our conversation here is simply to offer permission to risk joining us on the journey. At the end of the day, we are where we are because we decided in our hearts to make an intentional choice to come out of the shadows and risk telling someone the truth, allowing others to journey with us as we explore effective steps toward walking out a greater sexual integrity.

No matter where you are or how long you've been on this journey, we want you to join us.

3

THE MENTAL PATHWAYS OF MEN

For we are not unaware of [Satan's] schemes.

2 CORINTHIANS 2:11 NIV

"Oh, you're a very bad man!"
"Oh, no, my dear. I . . . I'm a very good man—
I'm just a very bad Wizard."

THE WIZARD OF OZ (1939)

■■✝■■

Think back to how you felt when you first had clarity about your calling as a Christian leader. What thoughts did you have about how ministry was going to be?

Chances are, you didn't give much thought to the potential problems or risks associated with such a calling. You had a heart for preaching, evangelism, organizational leadership, missions or bringing some revolutionary new product or service to the Christian marketplace. Your sights were locked on riding shotgun with Jesus to change the world.

MISSION ON THE DARK SIDE OF THE MOON

So what happened along the way? I'll tell you what: reality set in. It's not that our passion changed or even that we became jaded in our calling. It's kind of like getting married. The euphoria of puppy love propels us into a relationship—even good and God-honoring ones—but necessarily burns off after the booster rockets break off. What we're left with are the smaller thrusters to navigate our tiny space capsule in zero gravity. We also quickly became aware of the dangers of asteroids, debris and space junk in the cold of deep space.

I once worked with a church planter who was initially supported by his denomination to do work in an underserved area. From the outset, he was excited to have the opportunity not only to reach the lost but to use his love for the outdoors to create all sorts of outreach to the people in this rural location.

But as time passed, the daily grind of leading a church dragged him down. Relational conflict, financial concerns, reduced support from the denomination (financial and emotional) and the related marital stress all started taking their toll. Feeling isolated and uncared for, he begin feeling discouraged and abandoned. He also questioned whether God had really led him to the work in the first place.

Sometimes ministry is like working on the dark side of the moon. Unless we have seasoned encouragers reminding us what's happening, we can sometimes begin to doubt the existence of the sun when we no longer experience its warmth.

Let's step back a minute to regain perspective. There's a sinister design to this sort of struggle.

REMEMBER WHY WE STRUGGLE

You know the story. Envious of God's glory, Satan rebelled and lost the fight. For whatever reason, God didn't put him down right then and there, but left him to fight another day. We know his ultimate defeat *will* happen. But living now in the "time between the times"— that space in World War II between D-day and V-day—we contend with persistent and insidious guerrilla warfare from an enemy that refuses to accept defeat.

This ongoing assault has taken out many a good comrade along the way. In the early days of pursuing our calling, passionate ministry can sometimes blind us to the realities of spiritual warfare in Christian leadership. Discouragement becomes something unexpected rather than an essential conflict we all face at times. When unexpectedly confronted by discouragement, we become susceptible to burnout and moral failure.

Actually, we're not even Satan's ultimate target. His real focus is to embarrass or tarnish our King's reputation. It's a personal vendetta against his former Commander. And as jaded men sometimes do after being fired, he's gone postal. But since God's too big a match for him directly, he did what any scheming and intelligent adversary would do.

He turned to the King's kids.

WHY OUR SEXUALITY IS A PRIME TARGET

As his kids, we reflect God's image in lots of ways. Our intelligence, our will to choose and our bent toward creativity are just a few that come to mind. But at the core of that reflected image is our gender and our sexuality:

> So God created mankind in his own image,
>> in the image of God he created them;
>> male and female he created them. (Gen 1:27 NIV)

This verse is a striking biblical example of what's known as synthetic parallelism and chiasm in Hebrew poetry. In each line, the same truth is presented three different ways (see fig. 3.1).[1] With this visually mapped out, it's easier to see what was obvious to the early biblical readers: the essence of God's image is manifest in

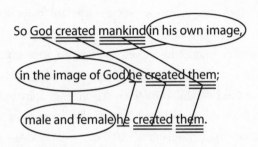

Figure 3.1. Poetic structure of Genesis 1:27

the creation of male *and* female. Neither gender alone sufficiently reflects that image. While plenty of other important conclusions can be drawn from this, clearly our gender (male and female) and the union of our genders (our sexuality) is at the very heart of our representation of God's image.

Why, then, should it surprise us that Satan's number-one target in the twenty-first century is both our gender and our sexuality? Sure, sexual temptation has been used as a weapon against the church from its beginnings. But have you noticed how preoccupied we've become as a society with our sexuality—and the free and varied expression of it—since the sexual revolution? With each passing decade, there seems to be a new expansion of manifestations forming the front lines of spiritual warfare against God's image in his creation.

The more our enemy can keep us selfishly preoccupied with issues surrounding our sexuality, the less focused we'll be on reflecting his image to others, especially to those who are spiritually lost.

GENERAL RISK FACTORS FOR MEN

In many ways, men and women are equally susceptible to sexual temptation. Historically, women tend to be more vulnerable through emotionally and relationally oriented sexual temptation, while men tend more toward the visual and physical. This seems to be shifting in recent decades, resulting from both the masculinizing of femininity and the feminizing of masculinity. In short, our enemy is attacking God's image at the root by trying to stamp out our uniquely masculine and feminine imprint. If male and female are no longer distinct, the metaphor of God's image represented in our separate genders and within the male/female marital relationship also ceases to exist.

But when it comes to men in general, here are a few vulnerabilities men tend to exhibit when it comes to sexual temptation:

Frozen *(the problem of a disconnected heart).* Those of us with preschoolers are helplessly immersed in the Disney franchise of movies. It's just too steeped in their cultural world. Our family doesn't even own the movie *Frozen*, but that doesn't stop our three-year-old daughter from wandering around the house singing at the top of her lungs, "Let it go! Let it GOOOOOO . . .".

And it's driving me crazy. I've actually been surprised to discover most people's lack of connecting the similarity between Elsa's "power" to freeze everything she touches and the "power" that compulsivity or addiction has over people's lives. Her inability to control this power ultimately causes her to retreat and live in isolation.

In my view, the "Let It Go" song clearly illustrates life in the throes of addiction, from hiding and dissociation ("Conceal, don't feel, don't let them know") to the delusional confusion that her chains actually represent freedom ("No right, no wrong, no rules, for me I'm free"). Her final, show-stopping declaration before disappearing deep into the frozen forest alone is an expression of an addict in complete denial: "The cold never bothered me, anyway!" Perhaps the song might be more accurately titled, "Suck It Up."

If we only had a male Disney character to sing this one! After all, isn't that the message most of us received as boys—verbally and otherwise—from our dads and other men around us growing up? This is the global message of American masculinity. Such a nagging sense of failure, poor self-control, fear, isolation, hiding and living unaware of our emotions are common denominators among men. Perhaps these evidence why various addictions plague twice as many men as women.

No sweat (the problem of self-sufficiency). I have a Canadian client who once shared with me his perception about American men being rugged, self-sufficient individualists. We export this image around the world through Hollywood. The last hundred years are replete with images of male heroes that are self-reliant loners.

Interestingly enough, many of these characters feel generally misunderstood by others. Perhaps such misunderstanding is unnecessary, as heroes often only feel this way because they are unique, one-of-a-kind individuals. They fear being judged and ridiculed if known beyond their public persona. So they retreat into self-sufficiency and personal obscurity as a coping mechanism for survival.

Self-sufficient men live unaware that God created us for community. It's where we can be known, understood, and embraced for our uniqueness. Real community is also where we can do the most good for one another. It's no less true for Christian leaders.

The proud wizard (the problem of pride). One of the iconic movies of the twentieth century is the *Wizard of Oz.* The wizard is regarded by everyone as an all-powerful, larger-than-life character. But he's no match for little Toto, the lapdog who pulls back the curtain to reveal a frail and timid man who seems powerless to deliver any of his grand promises. Like many men in Christian leadership, he admits to being a "good man . . . just a very bad Wizard."

But here's an interesting observation about the wizard. While he only displays a façade of power from behind his curtain, he discovers an ability to truly impact others once he's known for who he really is in life-on-life community with others.

I find this to be true of men more often than not. When out of fearful pride we isolate and become self-sufficient, we project an image toward others like that of a blowfish—a bigger-than-life persona as a defensive coping mechanism for survival. Most who see our exterior misinterpret its meaning. Either they are codependently drawn toward our veneer of strength or offensively repelled away from us as self-absorbed egotists.

Yet in reality, most of us are simply little boys who are physically all grown up but who still struggle to internalize a solid, masculine identity.

Shipwrecked (the problem of isolation). When we're disconnected from our emotional self—as most of us were taught by the previous generation—we live with few, if any, meaningfully close relationships. So while we might participate in jobs and recreation leagues and church groups where we enjoy spending time with hundreds of folk, we still feel isolated and alone. We may rub shoulders side by side with other men, but without the intentional and vulnerable disclosure of our real selves, our interactions with others feel more like Tom Hanks talking to his "friend" Wilson (the volleyball in *Cast Away*) than anything else.

This may account for why we often hate spending time alone with our own thoughts. The silence is deafening as we impulsively seek to fill the void with some sort of busyness that returns us to a feeling of normalcy.

A one-tracked mind (the problem of biological brain wiring). There's also something biological that contributes to our typical male struggles. One of my former therapist colleagues, Doug Rosenau, shares the analogy that a man's brain is like a chest of drawers, while a woman's brain is like an armoire.

Generally speaking, the sections of a woman's brain function in seamless concert with each other. Throw open the doors of an armoire, and we see everything simultaneously. While there are shelving and cubbies to allow for organization, everything is interconnected. Women benefit from quick decision making and an ability to see the bigger picture more readily. Of course, this can make things a bit messier, when stuff from different sections of the armoire (and a woman's thinking) spill over into one another.

By contrast, most men function by having categorical drawers from which to function. There's a work drawer, family drawer, fun drawer, sex drawer, spirituality drawer and so on. Unless two drawers are intentionally left open, we generally function from one drawer at a time. Even when multiple drawers are open simultaneously, there's still a structure and organization to things with minimal commingling.

This organizational style has its benefits, including simplicity, greater linearity and a general resistance to mental chaos. But a major drawback is the potential to live from only one drawer without an awareness of its impact on the contents of the others. This becomes especially critical to understand where sin is involved. In sexual sin, for example, a man's denial makes him unaware how such behaviors impact the other drawers of spouse, children and spiritual leadership. In fact, certain drawers over time have locks placed on them, with a key discretely tucked away from public access.

ADDITIONAL RISK FACTORS FOR CHRISTIAN LEADERS

Clearly we have our challenges as men. While we inherited these problems from previous generations, we must accept full responsibility for how we choose to live as men today. Yet, there are a few added problems common to men serving in Christian leadership:

The buck stops here (the problem of being at the top). "Leaders are like eagles. They don't flock; you find them one at a time." This is a favorite saying in leadership, but the truism has a clear downside. As an honest CEO knows, inherent problems exist at the top of the food chain. Lack of real accountability and oversight are often an invitation for indiscretion, exercise of poor judgment and secret sin.

As a leader of teams and leader of leaders, it's often not appropriate to be completely candid and emotionally vulnerable with those we lead. However, many leaders take this too far. Just because it may not be appropriate to share intimate details with those who follow us doesn't mean there isn't a need for processing private and personal thoughts in some relationship *somewhere*. There's a difference between prudence in being publically guarded and wearing a mask in every setting as a part of our core identity of hiding.

Among Christian leadership (especially those who carry pastoral duties), there's the additional problem of confidentiality gone awry. By virtue of our ministry positions, confidences must be kept in the stories we hear from others to effectively enter their sacred space. But in our confidence-keeping role, we sometimes take on this sort of "sin eater" role as synonymous with who we are, wrongly assuming we're resigned to being intimately unknown in our own personal relationships.

What's necessary in the context of a ministry relationship is damaging and potentially fatal when withheld from a close friend, mentor or marriage partner. If we remain intimately unknown in our closest relationships, much of the transformative power for our lives and ministries will be lost.

King of the hill (the problem of standing in for God). It's no mystery that we serve as God's representatives in a fallen world. Yet this position creates tension from both sides of the equation. Instead of being seen as human leaders with feet of clay, the brokenness in those we lead sometimes causes them to degenerate into worshiping us instead. While this may be a bit overstated in many cases, it's certainly not in others.

As with ancient Israel, people sometimes want a king rather than to follow the One who already is.

On our side of things, we secretly crave attention from those we lead. Many seminarians, in addition to legitimately wanting to partner with God to change the world, pursue ministry as a way to repair feelings of insignificance and lack of childhood affirmation. In effect, we want to be king as much as others want us to be. This is a dangerous combination in ministry.

The paparazzi (the problem of being celebrated). Well-known by everyone, but known well by no one. This is the problem of celebrities and Christian leaders alike. Most leaders are winsome influencers. This has nothing to do with being an introvert or extrovert, but more about that innate quality that causes people to like us and want to trust us. Perhaps this is further reason why we tend toward pride and narcissism.

Of course, such influence is a tremendous good when unselfishly used on behalf of the kingdom. But when it terminates in our own kingdom, we become more like vain Hollywood celebrities who seek the camera for public attention to support a pet cause (which often turns out to be nothing more than our own ego).

WHAT'S THIS GOT TO DO WITH SEXUAL TEMPTATION?

These manhood and leadership challenges make us more susceptible to various forms of temptation—sexual temptation, in particular, because of its relational orientation. As men, we were created to be just as relational as our female counterparts, though this isn't obvious based on how most men live. While we may express this more in terms of physical activity than conversation, for example, we're still no less relational.

When this relational nature isn't given healthy expression, it goes underground and finds indirect, unhealthy ways of expression. Pseudorelational expression, if you will. Such disordered expressions represent the various types of sexual temptation we men face. This seems especially true of pornography, due to its ubiquitous availability and seemingly anonymous accessibility (it's a complete lie, but our believing this facilitates our pursuit of it all the more).

THE TYPICAL MALE RESPONSE

Okay, so what if most or all of this is true? Now what?

Well, the typical next step for most men is rather predictable. We tend to sing a stanza of "Suck It Up," hide behind the wizard's curtain and push ourselves to create a linear, performance-based self-improvement plan to stop any and all vestiges of sexual temptation in our lives. Period.

After all, this is what we were taught to do as men, right? Regardless of how good or bad we are at such self-improvement plans, it's what most of us feel driven to do. It's the way our fathers did it or, at the very least, the way they told us to do it (as we well know, some of them were very poor models).

Yet if we're honest, we know where this leads because it's a well-worn path. While it does result in some degree of behavior change on the outside, the change isn't sustainable. And we still feel awful about ourselves on the inside, mostly because the motivational tool we use for change is shame: "What's wrong with you? Get your act together! I can't believe you screwed up again! You need to get back closer to God so this doesn't happen again. One more mistake like this and you'll lose it all!"

Notice how these statements sound like they're coming from outside of us? They are. They sound like our voice, alright. But it's another clever parlor trick from the enemy. Our voice, his words. Often we've heard these words before, perhaps from a critical parent, teacher or coach. But ultimately, messages of condemnation come from our enemy (Rom 8:1).

Most of us didn't grow up recipients of very much grace. Even those of us who grew up in Christian families are more familiar with a performance-based model for behavioral change than a grace-based one that leads to true, heart-driven transformation over time. It's a distinction that deserves a bit more attention.

4

THE GRACE-BASED PATH

A gentle answer turns away wrath,
but a harsh word stirs up anger.

PROVERBS 15:1 NIV

Come to me, all you who are weary and burdened,
and I will give you rest. Take my yoke upon you and
learn from me, for I am gentle and humble in heart,
and you will find rest for your souls. For my yoke is
easy and my burden is light.

MATTHEW 11:28-30 NIV

■■✝■■

"Dad, can I help you work on the car?"

"Sure. Let me do this first, and then you can help."

Eight-year-old Johnny sat in anticipation, excited to be able to help his dad with a big-boy project.

"Ok, now hand me that wrench." Unsure which one he meant, Johnny gave it his best guess.

"No, not that one, the other one! *Now*, before all the oil drains out!" Dad snapped angrily, as if Johnny had given him the wrong wrench on purpose. Johnny swallowed hard and handed his dad the other wrench, trying to ignore Dad's cursing under his breath.

"If you're gonna help, you've got to do what I tell you and not mess around!"

At that, Johnny's heart sank. He turned and walked back into the house before his dad saw the tear he was choking back. Otherwise, Dad would grimace and huff in disapproval.

WHERE WAS GRACE?

There's nothing wrong with helping a child understand the connection between performance and consequences. "Eat your vegetables and you can have dessert." "Since you got a C on the test, you won't be able to go out this weekend so you can focus on your studies." Children need to understand the world as a relatively predictable place where consequences follow choice.

But many of us grew up in homes where grace was an all-too-uncommon experience. When we fail to receive positive affirmation about who we are and about how we are loved by key people independently from our behaviors, we grow up making the unconscious connection that we earn and lose acceptance of those relationships based solely on the quality of our performance. Such assumptions only make sense in the absence of positive affirmation of who we are.

Also, many children grow up in a world without lasting commitment to anybody for anything. Nothing is permanent. Employees rarely retire with the gold watch after thirty years of loyal service. Parents divorce as often as they stay together. Even toys are manufactured as disposable, just like many of a child's relationships seem to be—whether from moving cross-country or simply "moving on" to another friendship. And even though Dad moved out, Mom moved on to a new boyfriend and moved us to another state, and our girlfriend broke up with us for a football player, we're supposed to believe in a God who loves us for who we are, no matter what? It's no wonder we grow up confused about whether anyone can be counted on in life.

So in a world where relationships aren't permanent and the ones we do have seem to be kept and lost based on our performance, there are two choices: either we actually perform well to gain acceptance or hide our flaws and failures so we'll still get acceptance anyway. The first option leads to compulsive perfectionism; the second leads to hiding, lying and deceit to make others perceive us as better than we know we really are.

As we grow up, this has direct implications for our struggle with sin. Without grace, we tend to hide our sin. We lie and minimize. We blame others and our circumstances. To keep ourselves in line, we become harsh with ourselves as a way to prevent rejection by others. Our internal dialogue perpetuates the same performance-based acceptance we received as children.

THE PROFESSIONAL MINISTRY MASK

This is the experience of many children. Boys in particular experience this, because our society expects boys to have it more together than girls. But as we discussed in the previous chapter, Christian leaders have additional challenges in receiving grace.

First, we are professional grace givers. That is, it's a one-way giving relationship from us to those we serve. Generally speaking, the giving doesn't flow back in our direction. That's not the way professional relationships are designed to work. As a licensed professional counselor and certified coach, I might share certain life challenges with my clients, but I wouldn't disclose in real time my deepest pain. This would disrupt their ability to receive from me what they so desperately need.

Similarly, when a Christian leader has a deep need (especially one dealing with an area of hidden struggle), the average church member or ministry participant would have difficulty walking through this with him, as it distracts their ability to receive ministry from him as a professional.

Remember the problem of leaders being at the top? Things flow from the top down, not from the bottom up. Again, this doesn't mean those at the top don't have human struggles, like everyone else. It simply means they'll need to find other places for those struggles to be effectively addressed.

Second, some of us gravitated toward a life in ministry as an unconscious means to vicariously experience grace. For example, if we were homeless at some point as children, we might have gone into ministry related to helping homeless children, in part, to allow the "homeless child" inside us to be soothed as we minister to kids today. This is a great way to redeem our sufferings in a way that benefits others. But it's still different than (and not as healing as) someone ministering to us as a direct recipient of grace.

Finally, grace may be difficult for us to receive because we have unconsciously taken on our professional grace-giving roles as an identity, extending grace to others as a diversion from having to think about our own human need for experiencing grace. As crazy as it sounds, this may be in part why we often feel uncomfortable when others extend grace toward us. We feel in control when we give to others and that has become our identity. Quite honestly, we feel embarrassed and needy when someone offers grace to us. For that matter, if we see their generosity through our lens of performance-based acceptance, we might even feel it puts us in a position of owing them something down the road.

For these reasons and more, Christian leaders often have difficulty acknowledging their need for grace and accepting it when offered by others.

Ben (the never-married up-and-comer from chapter two) was all too aware of the risks of letting anyone in. He'd seen the headlines of so many fallen pastors in his own denomination. So he resolved to make sure no one found out about his online preoccupations. When given the opportunity to teach, he divided God's Word with skill, even when the subject matter hit close to home. When others gave him encouraging strokes about the quality of his content, he nodded appreciatively and encouraged them all the more to remain steadfast in their faith. No one knew the real reason the message was so empathic and full of understanding. After all, he was preaching to his own heart.

This is an example of what I call the *pastor mask*, and most of us are guilty of wearing it. Some more than others. I'm not saying we should bare our soul to everyone. But baring it to *no one* results in greater feelings of isolation and shame, which often fuels more struggle with sexual preoccupation.

This is a dangerous place for Christian leaders and eventually leads to deeper discouragement. We need to be honest with ourselves about this tendency toward redoubling our efforts in our ministry as a subtle form of denial and, instead, embrace our own humanity and need for grace.

UNBURDENED—IT'S NOT WHAT YOU MIGHT THINK

"Take my yoke upon you and learn from me . . ." What teacher expects a student to perfectly apply something they just learned for the very first time, every time? As parents of preschoolers, how ridiculous would it be for me or my wife to expect perfect performance every time we taught them something new? Not only would that be an exercise in futility, it would break their young spirits to the point they'd stop trying altogether.

So when Jesus says we're to learn from him, isn't he implying that it's going to take time? Would he not expect us to make mistakes in the learning? After all, isn't that the point?

What might this imply about the grace-based path to sexual integrity?

Perhaps grace to

1. be human;

2. acknowledge our impulses and struggles with temptation;

3. make mistakes;

4. have a safe place and safe people to support us; and

5. share with safe people who can help shepherd us back to the path of integrity.

In short, the grace-based path is permission for Christian leaders to not be perfect and permission to acknowledge that sanctification applies to our lives, too.

"Come . . . all who are . . . burdened. . . . my burden is light." This is a very different kind of unburdening than we'd initially think and, on brief reflection, different than we might even want.

The idea of being unburdened conjures up images of running a full-tilt Olympic sprint without restraints, completely unencumbered. We certainly have this in store for us in heaven, but this isn't going to be our experience now. Instead, what we're offered here is the freedom to no longer have to pull the entire load ourselves.

What's the heavy burden we've been pulling?

1. Performing and people-pleasing for acceptance from others and ourselves

2. Religious piety to gain acceptance from God

3. As Christian leaders, doing both of these alone at the top

The yoke Jesus speaks of is that old-fashioned farming tool used to leverage the strength of oxen to till the farmer's land. In the metaphor, Christ offers us to join *his* yoke, meaning he not only offers to be our "yoke fellow" (a constant companion for the journey) but also to bear the brunt of the load for us as the stronger ox.

Note that the burden isn't absent, but rather "light." What, then, is the nature of the weight of this new, lighter burden? It's the weight of

1. remaining in the yoke (similar to the abiding in the vine concept of John 15); and

2. surrendering to his path and the work he wants to do in and through us.

Trying to pull in a different direction than he's going will result in chafing and pulled muscles—not from doing the work but from the yoke itself. In this sense, true freedom comes from a different place than we'd expect. Our natural mind thinks freedom comes from one of two endpoints: either the complete indulgence of our sin or else the complete unrestraint from any sin struggle at all. Instead, Jesus says true freedom comes from the "light and easy" work of being in the harness alongside him.

Incidentally, Jesus says he's "gentle and humble in heart." This means he's not going to say, "Get it right or else," then punish, verbally shame or withhold something good (like we might have experienced in childhood). Rather, he gently whispers, "I love you and I'm sorry you made a harmful choice. How can I help you bandage this up and get back on your feet again?"

Note the implications for how we treat ourselves here as well. If we're going to be harnessed with Christ, we need this same gentleness and humility with ourselves, especially when we feel the burden getting heavier again from not following his lead.

While this has application for every believer, would this somehow apply any less to the Christian leader? Of course not. However, except for unique situations, this likely can't be played out publicly in real time in front of our congregation or the ministry participants we lead. As Christian leaders, we need support from those who understand our unique situation and are willing to extend grace as we imperfectly work through things.

Practically speaking, each of us needs *at least* one person we can reach out to for such support. This is a safe person who can be cultivated for such a purpose. If we don't have one, we may need to pay for one. Professionals like me exist for a reason. It can be expensive, but lack of support in a critical time can be even more expensive, costing significantly more than just dollars. Think about it: What's the price of a lost marriage partner, visitation to kids on the other side of the country or the complete loss of decades of ministry investment?

It's that important.

THIS IS SANCTIFICATION

God's in the business of loving his kids, no matter how poorly we perform. That's not a license to purposefully engage in sin or do something stupid, of course. But it is the grace-filled message Jesus extended to the woman caught in the act of adultery (Jn 8:1-11). Not, "Go and sin no more, then I'll forgive you," but "I forgive you. Period. Now from the safety of knowing you're not going to lose me or my love for you, go and sin no more." The first response would cause us to work harder for our redemption in a desperate attempt to earn a right to be in relationship with him. The second response guarantees us an unconditional relationship with him, one that challenges us to feel different about ourselves because he does.

This message sometimes takes a long time to sink in from the decades of trying to measure up with Dad and with God. But once it does, it has the power to radically transform us from the inside. Such transformation doesn't happen all at one time. Instead, Jesus takes us where we are in our messiness and gently leads us, step by step, down the path that makes us look more and more like a reflection of him. This is the essence of sanctification—even for the Christian leader. I'm certainly one who's been gradually transformed by grace over the past decade or so and it's changed my life. Notice I didn't say it *has* perfected my life. I *am being* perfected, a process that won't be complete until I see Jesus.

It won't be for any of us.

WE'RE IN THIS TOGETHER

Pornography and other sexual temptations have been Satan's perfect secret weapon for millennia among Christian leadership. Yet this seems more true in recent decades—especially since the advent of the Internet. Actually, it's perfectly tailored as a trap for the Christian leader. Who else has such privacy, time alone, lack of accountability, a presumption of integrity by others and isolation from close friendships than the typical minister?

And of course, we feel we can't tell anyone about our struggles, no matter how big or small those struggles are. We can't tell our boss, or we'll be fired. We can't tell our spouse, or she'll leave us. We can't tell our denominational advocates, or we'll lose respect or lose our ministry. We can't tell the leaders who work for us, or they'll try to push us out. We can't tell anyone within our ministry or church, or they'd stop following our leadership. We can't tell our close friend, because 70 percent of us don't even have one.[1]

I'm not saying there isn't a significant truth to this line of thinking in certain cases. But Satan wants us to draw the ultimate conclusion that this means we should *never* consider any of these avenues and that it confirms that we're destined to suffer alone, simply because we are Christian leaders. So the cycle continues and worsens with time.

It's the perfect huckster's racket, one we'll always lose.

I've heard it said before that when men reach somewhere around middle age, they often transition from a quest to build things to a desire to leave a legacy. Nearing the half-century mark, I want to leave a legacy to the next generation of Christian leaders. Frankly, I'm sick and tired of seeing the carnage of our ranks littering the roadway from our inability as a leadership culture to have honest dialogue about our common struggle with sexual integrity.

Together, if we can impact even a small countercultural group of Christian leaders, we could shake up the entire conversation and radically improve the impact of the Christian church in our day.

But if we're going to change the conversation among our peers in Christian leadership, we first need to have a conversation about *ourselves*. Because transforming culture—whether it's human culture, Western culture, Christian culture or the culture within Christian leadership—begins with personal transformation inside you and me.

To do that, we need to pack a few key provisions for the journey ahead. While each of these apply to the Christian life in general, we'll apply them specifically to the Christian leader's journey toward greater sexual integrity.

Let's start with our most basic provision: the discipline of surrender.

5

THE DISCIPLINE OF SURRENDER

Daniel: (practicing blocks in Mr. Miyagi's boat)
When am I gonna learn how to punch?

Miyagi: Learn how to punch after you learn how to keep dry!
(rocks the boat, throwing Daniel into the water)

THE KARATE KID, 1984

God opposes the proud, but gives grace to the humble.

JAMES 4:6

Consider it a sheer gift, friends, when tests and challenges
come at you from all sides. You know that under pressure,
your faith-life is forced into the open and shows its true
colors. So don't try to get out of anything prematurely.
Let it do its work so you become mature and well-
developed, not deficient in any way.

JAMES 1:2-4 THE MESSAGE

But the fruit of the Spirit is . . . patience . . . gentleness, self-control.

GALATIANS 5:22-23

■ ■ ✝ ■ ■

The words *disciple, discipleship* and *discipline* all come from the same root word. However, the root isn't based in some militaristic, "command-and-control" sort of thing. It's about being a pupil or an astute learner, which requires discipline from a mental and persistent-in-practice point of view. It's less about a sergeant barking orders to a young private and more about the judo instructor teaching his student how to subjugate his inner man to help him more effectively act according to his values rather than his fleeting and momentary impulses.

Less drill sergeant, more Karate Kid.

So when we use the word *discipline*, we're talking about the choices we make to intentionally live as disciples of Jesus. Remember, we're learning that for the yoke of Jesus to be easy and light we have to follow his lead and not pull against the direction he's traveling. The more we learn to live life his way and follow his lead, the easier and the lighter the burden becomes. For that matter, the less energy we expend on fighting against the yoke, the more energy we have to enjoy the benefits of being yoked with Jesus. That is, the more we have the ability to flourish in the Christian life.

In recovery terms we, by necessity, must focus on sobriety in our early steps along the path. Abstinence from pornography, alcohol or some other substance or behavior is where we have to start. But at some point, we realize that merely not doing something falls far short of the abundant life Jesus promised. So we learn new skills for healthier responses to our former vices and day by day we establish a good track record for not engaging. Eventually, we're able to turn a corner and focus less on sobriety and more on serenity. That is, we're finally able to focus on abundance and thriving rather than just surviving day-to-day preoccupation with temptation. The primary focus becomes less about the *don'ts* of sin and more about the *do's* of discipleship.

So let's focus on a key provision necessary to achieve sobriety and stop the bleeding.

THE NECESSARY FIRST STEP

There are lots of things we can do when we realize we're under attack by the enemy: make a healthier choice, quote Deuteronomy to the devil, phone a friend, sing a favorite hymn. All of these are good things to do. But if these are the first things we do, it will turn into more of a self-help maneuver than a biblical response.

James 4:7 says we're to resist the devil. But notice the context: "*Submit yourselves therefore to God.* Resist the devil, and he will flee from you." Surrendering to the Lord *first* enables us to run into a strong tower for help in our time of need. Once we're in his presence, the Lord can either equip us for the battle (Eph 6:10) or fight on our behalf (Ex 14:14). He's the One who knows best if we should fight, run or stand our ground in a particular situation.

This approach, of course, requires us to be intimately connected with the Lord in order to receive his instruction. It's just one more way he reminds us of our dependency upon him.

In the practical growth of our sanctification, we may find early on that we fail more often than we succeed as we're learning to recognize negative emotional states and our need for his help. I often give a practical example to my sexual integrity recovery clients about how this plays out in the early goings of recovery. When we're tempted on a particular day to engage sexual sin, we may not recognize our need for surrender until after we've given in to the temptation. When we come to our senses an hour later, it's not too late to pray a prayer of surrender.

Just because it's more beneficial to surrender before we sin (certainly in terms of avoiding the consequences) doesn't mean it's not beneficial to surrender afterwards. It's always appropriate to surrender to the Lord, since this is the whole point of salvation in the first place. Surrender after sin is still surrender, and provides significant training for our brain to more automatically act according to our values rather than our fallen impulses the next time we're tempted.

It's similar to the reason a football team watches video of the big game they lost the previous weekend. It's too late to win the game, but it's never too late to build the discipline of improving their game. That's exactly how it is with the practical work of sanctification in the Christian's life.

WALKING OUT SURRENDER

So let's discuss some practical interventions in the initial stages of surrendering on the path to greater integrity.

Remember our fellow journeyman Daniel, the former alcoholic-turned-Christian speaker? He traveled extensively for his work until his wife discovered the woman's email scrawled on a napkin in his blazer. While he'd experienced good recovery from alcohol, that never really trickled down into practical application in his interactions with women on the road.

In our work together, we realized early on that we could borrow from his past learning in his Twelve-Step community and leverage it in his new sexual integrity recovery. Here are some of the tools Daniel found most helpful in the early months of his recovery path:

A daily pledge. This is a true statement that can be reviewed or recited daily as a way of focusing our attention on the goal of sexual integrity. For Daniel, this included the Sexaholics Anonymous Daily Sobriety Renewal Pledge and the full version of the Serenity Prayer.[1] Other men have used tools such as a list of thirty motivations for staying away from the behaviors they've rejected (for example, "I don't want to hurt my wife," "I know porn supports the sex slave industry," etc.)[2] or a relevant verse from Scripture (such as Job 31:1, "I made a covenant with my eyes not to look lustfully at a young woman," NIV). One client even wrote a personal letter to himself reminding him of seven different character qualities the Lord had spoken over him and how his sexual sin resulted from his losing focus on the unique man God made him.

The Three Circles.[3] This adaptation from Sex Addicts Anonymous' classic model is a simple, visual way for seeing our overall integrity plan. Three circles are drawn like a target, with a red inner circle, yellow middle circle and green outer circle. Here are definitions of each, along with examples from Daniel's diagram:

Red = Choices to avoid because they are inconsistent with God's design

Yellow = Not inherently inconsistent with God's design, but they represent a slippery slope for us (those choices we know have a high degree of certainty for us that, if engaged, tend to slide into the gravitational pull of the red zone)

Green = Healthy and God-honoring choices we desire to prioritize that proactively build us up, leaving less bandwidth for wasting on yellow and red zone choices

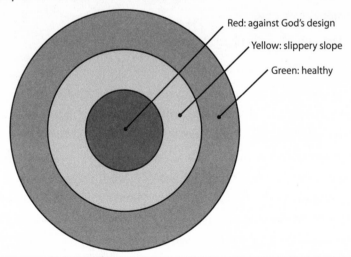

Red: against God's design

Yellow: slippery slope

Green: healthy

Figure 5.1. The Three Circle Method

Daniel's diagram included

Red:

- Pornography
- Any sexual contact with another woman
- Masturbation[4]

Yellow:

- One-on-one physical or social contact with a woman while traveling
- Watching television after my good-night call to my wife
- Taking an intentional second look at a well-dressed woman
- Perusing the magazine aisle at the airport

Green:

- Meditation on my daily pledge throughout the day
- A "last call" to my wife in the evening
- Time with God at 6 a.m. (using material *not* related to my professional speaking)
- Daily check in by phone with my Twelve-Step sponsor
- One additional Twelve-Step contact by phone or text

Longtime sex addiction recovery expert Dr. Mark Laaser uses the acronym LAMP for the red zone, which stands for "Lying, Affairs, Masturbation, Pornography." This is helpful for many as a constant reminder of the destructive nature of deceit and its devastating impact on our most important relationships.

Boundaries. Each of these circles represents an application of boundaries. The red and yellow circles represent boundaries for keeping bad things out; the green circles represent boundaries for keeping good things in.[5] Strong limits are a significant part of any sanctification process, but boundaries are only as good as our inner man is strong enough to respect them. We may need the help of others to encourage our respecting any limits we set. Our intimate relationships can encourage and provide accountability for these boundaries (more on this relational component later).

Other boundaries Christian leaders have implemented in their circles include providing pastoral counseling only in a room with a window in the door, not surfing the Internet after a certain time at night or only watching the TV shows intended rather the channel surfing. A person's boundaries can be as unique as the person setting them. We simply need to be honest with ourselves about what we really need that would be healthy for us, remembering Scripture's encouragement that even if something is permissible, it's not necessarily beneficial (1 Cor 6:12).

One additional boundary Daniel implemented was a ninety-day moratorium on travel. This allowed time for him and his wife to focus on rebuilding trust with one another, for Daniel to engage recovery coaching and for them to do some couple recovery work together. During this time, he avoided the Internet for the most part, and once his travel started again, he installed an Internet monitoring service for all his electronic devices. Because he wanted complete transparency with his wife, he added her name to the list of recipients for that report alongside that of his sponsor and support group buddy.[6]

Software for filtering/monitoring. This is a common boundary for men with Internet pornography struggles. Software is available for computers as well as most electronic devices. There are two types. *Monitoring* allows another man or group of men to see everywhere we go on the Internet (the URL addresses, not an image of the actual webpage). Within accountable relationships, this is enough information to allow them to say something to us if they see concerning things in our history. When that man is someone we care about, we're willing to let them graciously help us to improve our behavior online. *Filtering* places restrictions on access to certain webpages the filter deems likely to be pornographic or inappropriate. Phones and tablets have applications that provide similar services, although a workaround must generally be done to make them most effective. All programs have inherent drawbacks, but the benefits outweigh the disadvantages of not having it for those who use it. Examples include CovenantEyes.com and X3Watch.com.

Relapse prevention plan. This is a written document containing all the recovery action steps engaged with any degree of regularity, such as those we engage daily, weekly, monthly or periodically (intermittent travel, for example). Daniel included his concentric circles diagram, the support group he attended, names of his primary accountability buddies in the group (first names only, since they were from the support group) and the names of two books he was reading related to his integrity recovery.

This document can be helpful for sharing with a recovery group for transparency in our recovery path. It can be especially helpful to share with our spouse. When she no longer trusts our words because of infidelity, she can watch our actions be exactly what we told her they'd be by comparing our relapse prevention plan with what we actually do moving forward.

Incidentally, Daniel and his wife contacted me for help without telling anyone else about his struggles. While this is how it turned out in Daniel's situation, this isn't the way it always happens. Sometimes clients or couples reach out for wise guidance from professionals and Christian ministries equipped to help. Sometimes, a spouse reaches out to one safe friend, one in whom she is fully convinced of their confidentiality because the relationship has been well-tried by history. Other times, a spouse may indiscriminately share what's going on with a couple of girlfriends and a version of the story leaks out through gossip. Or, a leader's behavior is discovered by someone on his board or someone within his denomination or ministry. These latter two scenarios nearly always work against a healthy recovery process for the leader.

Again, this is the benefit of having an experienced professional walk with a couple to create a tailor-made recovery plan that's not only healthy and wise but also consistent with the couple's actual values, instead of their reacting to impulses they may feel at the emotional impact of discovery or disclosure of the leader's sexual struggle.

RESISTING PRIDE, EMBRACING HUMILITY

These are only a few of the basic early recovery tools that can be used as practical manifestations of a Christian leader's willingness to surrender. Human pride motivates us to bury the problem, admit it to no one and clutch to our pastor mask for dear life. But James 4 speaks of God's resistance toward the proud. It's not just that he doesn't help. He *actively resists* us.

By contrast, he goes out of his way to give us grace when we humble ourselves.

What does choosing humility look like when we show a desire to walk a path of integrity? It begins with this idea of surrender. Implementing the suggestions here may be embarrassing, feel weak and could result in the loss of key relationships or employment. For some it does, for others it doesn't. It's like pleading no contest with the judge. We still might face consequences, but we also might get unmerited favor. But if we're guilty, we're certainly going to eventually suffer consequences by holding onto our pride and trying to plead our case before a Judge who knows better. Sooner or later, it's usually just a matter of time. It's only when we're in the middle of clutching our sins in secret that we're deceived into believing otherwise.

Our surrender to God is our most practical expression of humility. While I can't exactly say for sure what grace might look like in a particular situation, I can tell you many of my clients have experienced a better quality of life than they ever thought possible by taking this road less traveled—not necessarily at first, but as they continued on the path over the long run.

THE HUMILITY OF DISCLOSURE

One of the more consistent lessons I've learned in working with Christian leaders in this area is the hands-down benefit of disclosure over discovery. *Disclosure* is a voluntary sharing of our struggle and situation with someone who can help us. That person may be a professional, mentor, accountability buddy, spouse or whomever. Our choice to voluntarily share where we really are and to expose the dark places is a practical manifestation of laying down our pride and humbly choosing to invite God's grace. Yes, we'll have to deal with the consequences of our poor choices. But it communicates to those we tell that we really do want help and aren't going to actively resist any help they offer.

Not so with *discovery*. When a spouse discovers a woman's email address in her husband's pocket (as in Daniel's case), or a fellow employee sees pornography on our computer or an accountability buddy has to ask us about questionable searches they saw on our accountability report, we not only have to deal with the consequences of our choices but also the added mistrust that results from our lack of proactive disclosure.

In marital situations, I can confidently say that more marriages dissolve among my clients due to the mistrust from multiple discoveries than ever dissolve from the actual sexual infidelities themselves. Even in cases where the Christian leader continued to intermittently make poor choices after starting recovery, marital trust was rebuilt more frequently and more quickly when the leader consistently and proactively disclosed those choices moving forward than in cases where the spouse had to confront him time and again— even when the leader was completely truthful after being confronted.

As a rule, proactive disclosure *before* being confronted results in better recovery than telling the whole truth after being confronted— though the latter is still better than a half-truth or outright lying when confronted.

So the first and most basic provision for the road to sexual integrity recovery is surrender—the abandonment of our pride and a willingness to humbly walk the path in the first place. This is where the journey begins.

Once we're willing to come under Jesus' yoke and receive his grace, there are a number of other provisions that help sustain us along the way. They're all part of the rebuilding process and will be familiar to you as important disciplines in the Christian life. But they're especially important on the path to sexual integrity.

As Christian leaders, we tell others how important it is for believers to practice these disciplines. It's time to take an honest inventory of their place in our own lives.

THE DISCIPLINE OF
RADICAL HONESTY WITH SELF

There's one way to find out if a man is honest:
ask him; if he says yes, you know he's crooked.

MARK TWAIN

The heart is deceitful above all things,
and desperately sick;
who can understand it?

JEREMIAH 17:9 ESV

I'm increasingly seeing that I am not very aware of
the emotional aspects of my personality.

PASTORS SUMMIT PARTICIPANT,
QUOTED IN *RESILIENT MINISTRY*

■■✝■■

Ashley sat next to her husband, Matt, one of our fellow journeymen whom you first met in chapter two. He was obviously having a difficult time answering her question. "I just can't believe you didn't think about how opening that Twitter account might not be a healthy thing for you."

Matt sat with a blank stare on his face.

I asked, "Matt, what are you feeling right now?"

"I feel like she's trying to set a trap for me. I know it wasn't a good decision, but I'm having a hard time getting past her anger."

"Yes, but how do you feel?" I reiterated.

"Like the rug's been pulled out from under me."

"So, when the rug's been pulled out from under you, or you perceive a trap's been laid for you, *how do you feel*?"

After a long pause, he finally responded, "I guess I feel ashamed."

EMOTIONAL CRAYONS

As men, we often have limited emotional insight. Many factors influence this. First, our brains aren't as holistically connected as those of most women (think armoires and chests of drawers). Second, while women tend to be more external processors of emotion (processing verbally her surface emotions, then going deeper little by little as she talks it through), men tend to be more internal processors (requiring what I call "cave time" to first think something through deeply before sharing and processing those emotions with others). Third, we learned from our early influencers it is dangerous for boys to show weakness, and our emotions were considered by the culture an expression of weakness. Finally, when we spend most of our childhood disconnected from our emotions (positive and negative), we can eventually come to believe that we just aren't very emotional at all.

As a result, our emotional muscles atrophy from lack of exercise. By the time we reach adulthood, we've become accustomed to using a box of only eight emotional crayons to color our world: sad, mad, glad, happy, frustrated (which really is a shade of mad) and maybe a few others.

Actually, they sound more like an off-off-Broadway version of the Seven Dwarfs than feelings.

Girls, however, typically grow up without such emotional prohibitions. Many women use a huge box of 120 crayons, shading their world in all manner of emotional color. Combined with their holistically connected brains and tendency towards quick external processing of emotions, most women not only have good personal insight but also an enhanced ability to share that insight with others and receive helpful feedback.

THE PRESSURE COOKER

Perhaps the connection between sexual indiscretion and low emotional awareness isn't readily apparent for some of us. But anyone in recovery from serious addiction or other life-dominating problems would tell us such recognition transformed their recovery. Humans were created to experience a wide variety of emotions. It's yet another way God made us in his image. We're like an emotional pressure cooker, with various release valves for letting off steam. A primary release valve is the verbal expression of our emotions. In this way, God designed us to literally "ex-press" emotion.

When we aren't fully aware of our emotional state, it's not that we don't feel our emotions. Instead, those emotions (especially the negative ones) become trapped inside us and build up internal pressure. With the primary release valve inoperative, the emotional pressure either finds another release valve for expression (such as a facial expression or song selection on our iPod) or discovers some other path of least resistance for escape—including cracks in the cooker. These cracks can be anything from muscular tension to sleeplessness to withdrawing from others to changes in our appetite. Lacking insight about our real deficit, we may also reach out to any sin that offers promise of temporary satisfaction or escape.

It's important for us to take ownership of this deficiency and do what's necessary to improve our emotional awareness. When I first entered graduate school for professional counseling, I was surprisingly unaware of my own emotions. I found it much easier to understand the emotions of others than my own.

During graduate school and the few years that followed, I found it beneficial to tuck an emotional chart inside my journal. Whenever I became aware of a feeling but didn't know how to label it, I would pull it out and look over the emotions. For me, it was helpful to see a list of possible emotions for comparison with what I was feeling. Now, over twenty years later, countless clients have given similar beneficial feedback. I've included the emotions chart I use most often with my clients in figure 6.1.[1]

Another element to my "emotional recovery" was granting my wife permission to give me honest feedback about her observations of me. I was nearly forty years old when I got married, so I unfortunately had lots of time to operate in an emotional vacuum. With her encouragement, I reluctantly invited her gracious input whenever she noticed any of those nonverbal expressions I mentioned earlier. When my eyebrows furrowed or when I broke eye contact from her or when I seemed distant or expressed negativity, she would gently offer reflection back to me as a sort of emotional mirror.

True confessions here: on our best days, this is the way it worked. However, with any two fallen people, there were bound to be days where she wasn't as gracious in her approach or I wasn't as receptive to her grace. Sometimes, these resulted in a marital spat, of which there were more in the early years of our marriage than there are now. But despite those times of marital conflict, the process of becoming more deeply known has been totally worth it.

So first, we can give ourselves permission as men to have emotions. It's not like we don't have them anyway. Second, we can also give ourselves permission to *feel* those emotions. Instead of the common "suck it up" male response to negative emotions, what

FEELING WORDS

A Little → A Lot

Mad	Sad	Glad	Afraid	Confused	Ashamed	Lonely
bothered	down	at ease	uneasy	curious	uncomfortable	out of place
ruffled	blue	secure	apprehensive	uncertain	awkward	left out
irritated	somber	comfortable	careful	ambivalent	clumsy	unheeded
displeased	low	relaxed	cautious	doubtful	self-conscious	lonesome
annoyed	glum	contented	hesitant	unsettled	disconcerted	disconnected
steamed	lonely	optimistic	tense	hesitant	chagrined	remote
irked	disappointed	satisfied	anxious	perplexed	abashed	invisible
perturbed	worn out	refreshed	nervous	puzzled	embarrassed	unwelcome
frustrated	melancholy	stimulated	edgy	muddled	flustered	cut off
angry	downhearted	pleased	distressed	distracted	sorry	excluded
fed up	unhappy	warm	scared	flustered	apologetic	insignificant
disgusted	dissatisfied	snug	frightened	jumbled	ashamed	ignored
indignant	gloomy	happy	repulsed	unfocused	regretful	neglected
ticked off	mournful	encouraged	agitated	fragmented	remorseful	separated
bristling	grieved	tickled	afraid	dismayed	guilty	removed
fuming	depressed	proud	shocked	insecure	disgusted	detached
explosive	lousy	cheerful	alarmed	dazed	belittled	isolated
enraged	crushed	thrilled	overwhelmed	bewildered	humiliated	unwanted
irate	defeated	delighted	frantic	lost	violated	rejected
incensed	dejected	joyful	panic stricken	stunned	dirty	deserted
burned	empty	elated	horrified	chaotic	mortified	outcast
burned up	wretched	exhilarated	petrified	torn	defiled	abandoned
outraged	despairing	overjoyed	terrified	baffled	devastated	desolate
furious	devastated	ecstatic	numb	dumbfounded	degraded	forsaken

A Little → A Lot

Figure 6.1. Emotions chart

many of us need are tools and safe relationships that give us permission to admit life in a fallen world is intensely painful at times. Even Christian leaders need places to express and work through our raw emotions in healthy ways and relationships of nonjudgment.[2]

While I'm certainly not suggesting we publicly shout these things from the rooftops, we don't have to overcorrect to the other side by pretending such feelings don't exist. Only harm comes to us when we use denial as a coping mechanism for our negative emotions.

WALKING OUT EMOTIONAL DISCIPLINE

Matt's overall passivity was partly due to his more introverted personality style. Left to his own devices, Matt (the nonprofit director with the special delivery) had the tendency to be more reclusive when he wasn't encouraged otherwise. This tendency of keeping to himself, combined with his being the director of a nonprofit, was part of what fed his secret life. Had it not been for his mail-order pornography, he might never have been discovered.

On the downside, Matt lost his ministry position as a result of his choices. However, because he was pointed in the direction of professionals who knew how to help him, Matt's willingness to walk a formal recovery path (in his case, a residential intensive) was a critical element for encouraging Ashley to stay beside him in the early days of his recovery. She made no promises, but she felt a strong resolve to honor her commitment to the Lord in giving her marriage every possible chance to work out.

Here are some of the choices Matt put in place with regard to emotional disciplines.

Journaling. Matt placed the feelings chart in his Bible. Every day during his evening prayer time, he pulled it out and reflected on his feelings at various points throughout the day. When there was an emotion he thought his wife would appreciate knowing, he texted the feeling to her, as well as the reason for that feeling: "I felt content to realize I've been in recovery for over three months today"; "I feel encouraged every time you give me positive affirmations about my progress in recovery"; "I felt embarrassed today when a coworker at the grocery store where I work was surprised I used to run a Christian nonprofit."

Slowly but surely, Matt was integrating emotional language into his daily conversations. More importantly, he was becoming more aware of what he was feeling throughout the day, especially when a negative emotion still triggered his desire to reach out to a pornographic image. The more aware he became about his feelings, the more he realized his tendency to reach out for porn when he felt lonely, insignificant at work, "less than" in comparison with others in ministry and inadequate sexually with his wife. Somehow, the eyes of those in the porn always seemed to communicate that he mattered, he had what it took and that he was a man. Over time, he discovered he was more drawn by these deep emotional messages than he was from the actual sexual arousal he experienced.

When Matt found himself struggling with lust or temptation, he used his journal to document what was happening at that time ("preoccupied with going online for porn while my wife is out for the night"), his physical body sensations ("heart beating faster, butterflies in my stomach"), thoughts ("I wonder if she's coming back early tonight?"), feelings ("anxious, excited, scared, lonely") and the ultimate choice he made, healthy or not ("looked at porn" or "sent my wife an 'I love you' text and went for a brisk walk-and-pray around the neighborhood"). This gave Matt significant insight over time regarding the unique ways he struggled and, more importantly, how he could learn from his temptations in the future.

Daniel (the recovering alcoholic) also began journaling for the first time early in recovery. As he was naturally drawn toward the study of theology, Daniel tried to keep his journal entries as personal and application as focused as possible. He placed less emphasis on Bible passages and more on personal choices to walk as Jesus walked. For example, one month he used his journal to simply meditate on choices he could make to "take up his cross" by dying to self in his deliberate decisions to love God, his wife and his kids. "Clean one area of the house that needs it without complaining or being asked" was an example from his list.

Feelings feedback. Matt asked both Ashley and a close friend to help him become more insightful about his feelings. When he felt "bad" (an emotion he couldn't quite place), they helped him explore his true emotions by asking thoughtful and grace-filled questions, such as, "What did you perceive your boss was telling you when he said _____," or, "At what point in our conversation did you feel the sinking in your stomach and want to shut down?" This was especially helpful when Matt felt anger, as he'd learned over time that his anger was a surface emotion that often covered for deeper, more vulnerable emotions, such as feeling powerless, inadequate, small or threatened.

Family-of-origin inventory. Matt grew up in less-than-ideal circumstances, to say the least. His early relationship with both his mom (who was dominant and overprotective) and his dad (a larger-than-life, athletic, traditional masculine type) played a formative role in how Matt came to handle his emotions as an adult. As a middle child between two sisters, he grew up more familiar with feminine ways of handling life—except for his emotions. Those he kept under lock and key. He learned early on in a family of mostly women that emotions tended to get talked to death. "No thanks," Matt told himself. "I'll follow Dad's model of emotional stoicism on that one."

Of course, this wouldn't fly with Ashley, once they met and

married. In many a marital argument, Matt found familiar emotions resurfacing that seemed to belong more to the past than the present. And they did. Often, Matt had to use his journal to explore emotions of feeling powerless, controlled and manipulated, which belonged more to past interactions with his parents and siblings than to his bride, boss or friends in the present day.

Abuse inventory. Matt was sexually molested by an uncle for a brief time in kindergarten. This is something he never told anyone, not even Ashley. It only emerged once he started working with a professional who cared enough to ask the question outright. Honesty with the professional led to his eventual honesty with his wife. This disclosure led her to experience more empathy for Matt and softened her heart toward him. It didn't magically make his infidelity disappear, but it did help her perceive him as a vulnerable boy who'd been hurt along the way and had learned to cope with life in destructive ways. This change of perspective helped her to endure the long road of their recovery together.

Sexual inventory. To varying degrees, we've all made poor sexual choices in our past. We've suffered consequences—those we saw coming and those we didn't. Writing out a sexual history to share with one or more of our intimate relationships can help both us and them to work through our history. The inventory allows us to take greater responsibility and allows others with whom we share it the opportunity to be more empathic and understanding.

In the case of our wives, it can help them grieve the loss of expectations about who we've been and to know us fully. It also allows us to be known fully by our wives and to know that, if they choose to continue walking with us in full knowledge of our past, they are making an intentional choice to embrace us with full understanding—yucky parts and all. For those clients willing to take this step, it's one of the more powerful antidotes to their deep-seated shame. Such a risk in disclosure holds the power for serious freedom in recovery.

This was a vulnerable step for Matt, and took almost two months to deconstruct between us before he was ready to share it with Ashley. While she knew about the mail-order pornography, she didn't know the extent or the long-standing duration of his online porn history. Neither did she know about his abuse history or his sexual exploration with a couple of friends in middle school.

A few weeks postdisclosure (and unpacking these revelations with her own spiritual mentor), Ashley eventually came to disclose to Matt her own struggle with bulimia as a teenager—a story she'd never shared with him before. She never would have, if it hadn't been for his willingness to take the initiative in vulnerably sharing the raw truth of his own story.

Not every story works out this well, of course. But we'll never know the redemptive work God wants to do in our lives, our ministries and our marriages unless we're willing to take the risk.[3]

Triggers inventory. We're bombarded daily by people and circumstances triggering sexual lust and fantasy. For Matt, some of his triggers were on the outside, such as sexually oriented billboards or a boss who criticized his work. He was surprised to notice his triggers didn't have to be of a directly sexual nature to prompt a desire for engaging in a sexual solution (like Internet porn).

But sometimes his triggers came from within himself, such as discouragement over low ministry giving, exhaustion after a long day or disappointment over a friend canceling coffee. Matt started a working list of his more common emotional triggers: lonely, angry, tired, inadequate, controlled. Knowing these triggers helped increase his insight during future temptations. No longer as caught off-guard, he became more confident in his ability to choose a healthier emotional response than to reach out to a digital image for comfort.

Attentiveness. This refers to consciously accepting and not judging a particular thought or emotion. Within a Christian framework, attentiveness makes sense because we consider many of our thoughts and emotions as temptations rather than consciously chosen. When we aren't practicing attentiveness, we make the unconscious assumption these thoughts and emotions are our *choices*, blame ourselves for sinning and then experience shame from Satan when he whispers that these thoughts and emotions are merely extensions of who we are in our *identity as sinners*.

Attentiveness acknowledges these thoughts and emotions as *impulses*, but graciously allows us to reject them and to refocus on more God-honoring thoughts—without having to shame ourselves in the process. For example, in seeing a scantily clad jogger, Matt previously would jerk his head in the opposite direction and harshly tell himself, "I can't believe you just looked at her! You idiot!" But in time, he learned instead to tell himself, "Yes, she's attractive, but right now it's important to keep your eyes on Jesus," as he gently turned his head back to the road ahead. Seeing the jogger no longer held shame for him as he learned that seeing her the first time was not a sinful behavior on his part. Even if his gaze remained with her for an extra second or two, he learned that a more gracious response enabled him to refocus his attention without shame unnecessarily derailing his day.

Shame inventory. Most shame statements derive from our early experiences in childhood. Matt distinctly recalled hearing, "You'll never amount to anything" and "You'll never be as successful as _____." He also remembers his father's nonverbal huffs, his sister's comments about his husky pants and his mother's incessant questions about checking his homework "just one more time."

These become deep soul messages spoken into us by the words and actions of important people throughout our childhood. Hearing them only once or twice would be no big deal. But repeated ad nauseam, they speak deeply into our forming identity. Over time, these messages get reinforced by Satan's lies in our vulnerable moments as they take on fresh new meaning: "I can't do anything right," "I'm fat," "I'm stupid."

As Matt attended to these messages in his integrity recovery, he recognized themes developing and gave special attention to those sounding accusatory and condemning. He knew these came from the father of lies rather than from his heavenly Father.

Daily serenity tracking. Tracking serenity tasks in our green zone is a simple method for seeking to intentionally prioritize or improve healthy functioning in recovery, such as more frequent personal time with God, working out at the gym, going to bed on time, phone or text check in with a buddy, and so on. Some men track the same tasks daily; others track a different set of tasks unique to that day. There's no wrong way to do this.

Some of my clients do rather creative things with this. One used the back of his business card not only to write his top five serenity tasks, but also to reference his Scripture verse for the week to meditate on it throughout the day. Checking each task as he went along, he also placed a green check or a red "x" on the card, depending on whether he steered clear of porn and masturbation. He even tracked his running number of days since his last engagement of those behaviors—all on the back of his business card. He kept these cards in a safe place in his home office as a physical reminder of the work he was doing in partnership alongside God's daily grace for his journey (Phil 2:12-13).

Matt decided initially to put five daily serenity tasks on his tracking sheet: (1) engaging his evening quiet time, (2) journaling, (3) proactively sharing three emotions from the day with Ashley, (4) reasonable application of attentiveness throughout the day, and (5) praying with Ashley before bedtime. At the beginning of each day before work, he took five minutes to observe whether each had been done "well enough" the previous day—yet another way he practiced grace toward himself. This also allowed him a tool for reviewing the previous week every Sunday and gave him a more objective view into how well his recovery was going. More check marks tended to be connected with a greater feeling of serenity; fewer check marks generally seemed associated with a heightened vulnerability in his recovery. This also served as objective data for his wife and friend for their feedback.

Re-creations list (3 Rs).[4] Rest, recess and renewal: three tools for re-creating energy and vitality back into our lives. *Rest* is down time; *recess* is up time. *Renewal* is any intentional process engaged for the purpose of improving a skill or qualification over time.

For Matt, he'd always enjoyed reading and listening to audio books for restful activity. And, of course, there was middle-of-the-day power napping. But he neglected these before recovery due to the inordinate time he spent engaging porn. He also felt guilty for them, given his waste of time on porn. But now, he was learning to harness them once again for good reads and for when his brain needed a recharge.

As for recess, Matt was able to become more intentional about playing outside with his young son or dress up with his little princess. Hitting an occasional bucket of balls at the driving range was also a good way to release pent-up energy from work. For renewal, he was already searching for options to complete a doctorate of ministry. He also dreamt of completing a scuba certification to use on a future anniversary getaway with his wife.

"I feel hopeful about earning my doctorate," Matt said with a grin. "And I'm excited to dream about going diving someday with Ashley." He looked surprised at his own words and added sheepishly, "I guess I am making progress after all."

I smiled in agreement. Matt was trading his unhealthy fantasy for a healthy vision of the future.

CONNECTING EMOTION AND SPIRIT

When we're able to recognize and own our positive and negative emotions, we're able to know ourselves for who we are rather than seeing ourselves only for the masks we wear—whether it's our public "better than we really are" leader mask or the "worse than we really are" preoccupations of our unfaithful hearts.

When we're more honestly aware of our personal emotions, it's easier to recognize when we're in a dangerous situation and in need of asking the Lord for help.

7

THE DISCIPLINE OF
NONMINISTRY GOD TIME

We must never allow anything to damage our relationship with God, but if something does damage it, we must take the time to make it right again. The most important aspect of Christianity is not the work we do, but the relationship we maintain and the surrounding influence and qualities produced by that relationship. That is all God asks us to give our attention to, and it is the one thing that is continually under attack.

OSWALD CHAMBERS,
MY UTMOST FOR HIS HIGHEST (AUGUST 4)

But Jesus often withdrew to lonely places and prayed.

LUKE 5:16 NIV

■■✝■■

In late 2014, my wife contracted a particularly nasty type of food poisoning that landed her in our local hospital and also required a blood transfusion. Despite being cleared for discharge four days later, back home she experienced ongoing symptoms, including a troubling rate of fluid retention, breathing difficulties and intense day-long headaches. We had no idea what we were dealing with.

But sharing our hospitalization and post-discharge experience with her primary physician cued him to know exactly what was going on. He helped us understand that though her symptoms were alarming, she was experiencing the natural process of healing. (Wouldn't that have been nice to know on discharge from the hospital!) He also gave us a plan to follow for the next three to four days of her recovery.

Human emotions are much like the physical symptoms we reported to my wife's primary physician. Our ability to know what and where our emotional pains are helps us carry them to the Great Physician, readying our hearts for more receptivity to his "prescription," whether the nature of the remedies is emotional, physical, spiritual, relational or otherwise.

How long are we willing to remain sick (and potentially vulnerable to a spiritual heart attack) before we're willing to ask the Physician for help? My wife was acutely aware of her symptoms and sought out her physician as quickly as possible. Our Great Physician is available 24/7 and gladly takes every one of our calls personally. The more quickly we understand our vulnerable emotional condition, the faster we can call out to the One who heals our diseases (Ps 103:3).

FEELING THE TENSION

Now, a tension does exist between being fully surrendered to God and at the same time being fully alive and connected to our emotional state. The only way we can live in this tension is to be willing to grieve. Negative emotions are painful, and there's a reason why our fathers and our masculine culture taught us to be in denial about them. Nobody likes to sit with pain for no good reason, as evidenced by the multibillion-dollar market for painkillers.

Emotions are God's servants to tell us what's going on inside. Remember C. S. Lewis's quote about God shouting in our pain? God designed pain not only to tell us something's wrong. He also intends it as a practical means for grace through surrender of that pain to him.

That's actually what Jesus did on the cross by initially refusing the vinegar mixed with gall, which was offered to numb the pain. This, he refused. Later, Jesus requested his parched thirst be quenched (without the gall) so he could express what our hearts desperately need to hear, even today: "It is finished" (Mt 27:33-50; Jn 19:28-30).

It's this finished work of salvation that compels us to run to him. He understands our suffering and promises to be our lifeline in our times of need (Heb 4:16).[1] There's no shame in what we're feeling because Jesus already knows what's in our heart. He guarantees we won't be rejected, embarrassed, condemned or shamed. That's not his way. We have the confidence to gaze directly into his eyes and risk sharing our naked and most vulnerable selves with him.

WHO REFLECTS WHOM?

Intimate time with the Lord is of great value to all believers. However, it's easy to argue that it's more true for Christian leadership. In my own personal life as well as the lives of men I've walked alongside in recovery, it's surprising the ways we can excuse and even justify its neglect at times. As busy leaders, we often can allow our own ministry to become the "good" that crowds out the "great." How ironic that the thing to potentially damage our public ministry (other than blatant sinful behavior) might be neglect of the very thing our ministry is supposed to be built on.

There's nothing inherently wrong with spending our God time with content related to our sermons, writings or upcoming blog post. It's the direction of the flow that we're talking about as the problem. Are we using our God time to listen to the Spirit on a given theme and seeking to apply what we hear first to our own personal walk? This is consistent with allowing the Word to rightly divide our own hearts so a more powerful application of the gospel message can be applied through our ministry as Christian leaders. We go to God for direction, apply what we receive to our own hearts, then share it with others in light of its application to our own lives.

This is different than using our God time to research the Word for relevant ministry content and Scripture to back it up. This weakens our God time to nothing more than work, with the Word potentially bypassing our own hearts from meaningful application beyond the superficial. It's the difference between knowing the message and knowing the message in an intimate sense.

Are we going to the Word as our source of life, allowing the Spirit's ministry in our own hearts to overflow to others, or are we going to the Word for application to others only? Are we like the moon, reflecting God and his Word to others, or have we reduced God and his Word to the moon, reflecting *our* content?

When we read it in black and white, we can all agree this is a terrible idea. But in the busyness of our everyday leadership in ministry, it's just sometimes too easy to let things revolve around us instead of us revolving around him.

WALKING OUT SPIRITUAL DISCIPLINE

James (the rural pastor) would never have admitted his spiritual life was anemic. From all outside views, his life was in perfect order. The view from the inside, however, was a different story. The words were all right, but the heart was all wrong—and so were the behaviors no one else could see.

The church was in shock when James was arrested. Their surrounding community went through a season of confusion and disbelief. Could this really be happening in their small town? James lost his church and relocated his family to a larger city a few hours away for secular employment to provide financially. James and his wife were fortunate to find a Christian ministry that specialized in working with couples rebuilding from sexual brokenness. With individual support groups for both him and his wife, they were given the ability to take a deeper look inside their own lives for answers. For James, it was an opportunity to have others encourage him in applying God's Word to his own heart—not from the heady, theological perspective he was used to—but from a place he could finally admit the deepest of his shame and pain and allow God's Word to meet him in that darkest of places.

Here are some of the ways James began to apply spiritual disciplines in a more personalized way:

Personal God time. James often had difficulty experiencing spiritual nurture for himself, using his God times more for sermon preparation and blog research. When he lost his church, James struggled even having such times. But eventually, James allowed God into a very vulnerable place. Here, "God time" took on a whole new meaning.

It took nearly a year, but James eventually learned to allow his emotions to be "laid bare" in God's presence because he was now more fully aware of them. Crying was a more regular part of his prayer and Bible reading, too, as was his willingness to share what God was personally teaching him with his wife.

For Christian leaders still serving in ministry, the most powerful time we can invest is in our own spiritual life—time that's intentionally disconnected from our "official" ministry capacity. This isn't to say God can't speak a meaningful word for those we lead during our own personal time. As I mentioned earlier, it's just that God's message through our own prayer time and personal study of Scripture should be applied to our lives first, even if we see ready application to others from the moment God gives it to us. It may happen in a few moments or may take many months for the message to take root in us. But once it's done a work in us, it's ready to do a work in others.

I've seen this principle employed by pastors, songwriters, Christian speakers and Christian nonprofit directors alike. Once we're transformed, we then have a greater capacity to facilitate deep and lasting transformation in the lives of those we lead. We become a direct and unhindered conduit for God's grace to those we serve.

Lies inventory. On any given day before entering recovery, James told himself countless lies. "Just for a minute" and "it's not really porn" were examples related to his viewing of sexually oriented TV shows and videos. "She's irritable today, so I'm going to keep my distance" is an example of how passivity prevented him from loving his wife, as if her mood somehow gave him an excuse to not initiate toward her. "It's been a long day and I know she's not going to be up for anything (sexual) tonight. I'm going to see who's new on the dating site." This, coupled with "It's just talking," were all lies to suppress the Spirit's quiet conviction.

As we list lies we encounter throughout any given day, we'll usually notice themes. We can then ask God or another safe relationship for feedback about using truth to counteract such lies.

Theology of suffering. Suffering is an integral part of life. Often, James's sexual sin related to an attempt to seek pleasure or alleviate pain (or both) in ways inconsistent with God's plan for him. "Without realizing it, I came to unconsciously believe I could live in a world without suffering. My distorted thinking included thoughts like 'I deserve this' and 'it will help me refocus on my sermon preparation.' I was really messed up."

When James accepted life in this "sinful world as it is, not as I would have it,"[2] he came to admit that a certain amount of suffering is simply unavoidable. He gave himself permission to express his grief in different ways, rather than reaching out to sexual behaviors. This included honest expression of his griefs to the One who already knows them all too well, because he carried his very sorrow and bore his very grief (Is 53:4-5).

Stop and think about that for a minute. You may think your pain is unique and no one could possibly understand it. While I have walked through hundreds of stories similar to yours, there's none just like yours and there's no grief identical to it. That's true. In some ways I would understand, and in other ways I wouldn't.

But do you realize that Jesus knows the intimate feelings of your sorrow and the very personal details of your unique grief? I'm not talking about him knowing the facts of your trauma or difficult circumstances. I'm saying he *felt them* on the cross. Somehow, the God of the universe in the person of Jesus—with a human body and human emotions just like you and me—has, in a moment in time, felt the weight of your particular suffering.

Let that sink in for just a minute.

He feels the pain of your affair.

He feels the depth of heartache of the abuse you suffered for years as a child—a pain that, to this day, still no one knows.

He feels the loneliness of your absent dad growing up.

He feels your silent heart's cry surrounding your daughter's death as much as he feels the weight I carry daily in parenting my autistic son.

The wounds of Jesus now hold much more personal meaning for James. They can for us, too.

Other spiritual "disciplines." Scripture meditation, prayer, worship and solitude are but a few examples of disciplines beneficial to our spirit lives. We may have encouraged and led others in practicing these disciplines, but what about our personal experience of them? Taking time for a particular spiritual discipline—integrating it into our routines over a season of time—can revitalize our personal walks with God.

James had real trouble with corporate worship. No longer behind the pulpit, he felt out of place in the pews. But solitude was an area Jesus redeemed in his life over time. For most of his adult life, silence was something to avoid. That's when his old emotions would speak the loudest and he would sense a need to quiet them through spiritual busyness or sexual indiscretion. But James learned to sit with the silence. Such times became opportunities to spend intimately with Jesus. Sometimes Jesus would speak through the Holy Spirit and sometimes James would speak, too. Most of the time, they sat in silence together, especially when the weather was nice enough for him to be in the outdoors. The silence was no longer deafening, but nurturing. It was no longer something to be feared, but something to be embraced and even anticipated.

Scripture memorization and meditation. James searched Scripture for passages directly addressing sexual temptation, including familiar passages in Genesis 39, Proverbs 5–7 and 1 Thessalonians 4:3-8. He meditated on and memorized a few verses that spoke to him more personally. He studied larger passages through commentaries and other references—but this time applying them as God's Word directly to his own heart, with no one else in mind.

Periodically in our time working together, James would make comments about how the Holy Spirit brought to mind a personalized message from God during those times of intimate listening. When the Word takes on that level of personalization, recalling Scripture in times of temptation is no longer simply truth remembered. It's more like deep encouragement from a dad telling his son he's got what it takes to say no.

"He believes in me," James said, "and that makes all the difference in the world to me."

I CAN SEE IT

So far, we've seen the necessity of surrender for traveling on the sexual integrity path. We've also seen examples of emotional disciplines and how those are integral in being able to more personally apply spiritual disciplines to our lives as Christian leaders.

But the provisions we need for the journey aren't just intangible ones. Some of them have to do with our bodies. It may seem obvious, but we still need to talk about it. As we're both painfully aware, knowing and doing are two very different things.

8

THE DISCIPLINE OF
BODY MAINTENANCE

When we look at the Scriptures that talk about being holy in body and spirit, we just assume that's referring to our sexual ethics. Some of those Scriptures do, but not all of them. We're really the first generation that wears those blinders. Previous generations of the church were much more sensitive to honoring God by taking care of our bodies.

**INTERVIEW BY GARY THOMAS,
AUTHOR OF *EVERY BODY MATTERS***

You know the old saying, "First you eat to live, and then you live to eat"? Well, it may be true that the body is only a temporary thing, but that's no excuse for stuffing your body with food, or indulging it with sex. Since the Master honors you with a body, honor him with your body! God honored the Master's body by raising it from the grave. He'll treat yours with the same resurrection power. Until that time, remember that your bodies are created with the same dignity as the Master's body.

1 CORINTHIANS 6:13-14 *THE MESSAGE*

■■✝■■

You already know that it's inconvenient, time consuming and often expensive to give our bodies healthy maintenance. If you accept what I'm about to say here, you'll have to go visit the doctor for a physical, stop using the treadmill as a high-priced clothing rack, cut back or cut out those "Super Size Me" fries from Mickey D's, take medication you've been in denial about, and who knows what else.

Remember how pressure escapes through cracks in the cooker when we don't express our emotions in healthy relationship with others? Overeating, watching hours of television at night and getting only five hours of sleep are examples of cracks that in time erode our overall health. Stay on this slippery slope too long and we'll likely find ourselves making small—then eventually big—compromises in sexual integrity . . . if they aren't happening already.

BEN'S STORY

With great aspirations as an up-and-coming Christian leader, Ben (the never-married minister) had a number of things working against him. Like many, he cared too much about what others thought of him, whether ministry participants, coworkers, his mentor, his denominational leadership or young Christian women with marriage potential. And though his dad died when Ben was just a teenager, something inside him was just as driven to please him as ever.

Most of the time, he wasn't aware of these competing interests. But at a gut level, he was unconsciously burdened by the weight of it all.

Then, there's the way he'd always felt about his body. Ben's tall and slender build caused him to feel intimidated around more muscular men, especially those more knowledgeable of "masculine stuff," like fixing cars, hiking and building things. He'd always felt a bit like a poser around men like that.

Food was another unhealthy area for Ben. He got away with it because of his slender build. But he was drawn to caffeine and carbohydrates for a pick-me-up, and drive-thru fast food when he was under the gun of an important deadline (of course, it will still be another ten years before his waistline begins to show signs of this subtle form of self-abuse).

One other thing—not that anyone would know. Since his adolescent locker room days, he'd had a nagging inadequacy about his "size." This was added to his already strong preoccupation with his other previously mentioned inadequacies. His deepest fear was that he wouldn't please the woman of his dreams, physically or otherwise.

Ben wasn't aware of the connection between his strong sense of inadequacy, rejection from his dad (part Dad, part *perception* of Dad) and the resulting self-condemnation. This showed up in his negative self-talk, his compulsive work ethic and the nature of his pornographic interest.

In particular, he was drawn to pornography centered around women who inflict pain on men. This bent toward masochism fit his overall narrative, feeling the need for punishment for his inadequacies. This would be difficult for anyone in his public life to understand, as he came across as very confident and competent, especially in his ministry to others.

Ben and other overachievers like him function a lot like ducks. They look calm on top of the water, moving with proud confidence. But under the surface, there's a compulsive paddling that nobody ever sees. Like the pressure cooker, the public rarely sees how pressure gets released. But it escapes one way or the other, emotionally, spiritually or physically.

WALKING OUT PHYSICAL DISCIPLINE

It was obvious from early on this was going to be an area of focus for Ben. To his credit, he didn't need much convincing. He'd just never noticed any connection between his poor physical self-care and his nagging sense of self-condemnation. As part of his early assessment, we discussed his typical routine with regard to his general lack of body care.

Physical and blood work. "Doctor? What doctor?" Ben said matter-of-factly. "I'm never sick." But even when we're not sick, it's a good idea to have a regular physical, especially the older we get—at least every two years for younger folks, annually for those over forty. Physicians will usually order a standard blood profile to check things out generally, but if we're concerned about any level of lethargy, sluggishness or lack of zeal for life, we might consider asking for additional testing for testosterone, thyroid and vitamin D. Irregularity in these and other areas can mimic depression. Other possible culprits to discuss with a primary physician include medication side effects (especially antihypertensives, anti-Parkinson's, beta-blockers, corticosteroids, benzodiazepines), as well as recreational drug and alcohol use.

While we're having blood drawn, we might as well make sure it includes a PSA test for prostate cancer. It's a common problem these days and too many men die unnecessarily when it can be so well-treated with early detection.

By the way, some doctors may not realize that anger in men can be a symptom of male depression, especially when it's present with other symptoms, such as disturbances in appetite, weight change and sleep. We should be sure to mention this if we're prone to irritability and angry outbursts.

Ben's blood profile revealed deficiencies in both testosterone and vitamin D. Over-the-counter vitamin D supplements, along with a testosterone cream prescription from his doctor, contributed to a notable difference in his overall energy level.

Medication evaluation (general). If we've ever been recommended a medical procedure and not yet followed through, we might want to reconsider. It may be all right if we've not done so because we're pursuing other, less invasive options. But ignoring the problem won't do our bodies any favors.

Is the physician aware of over-the-counter medications or supplements that could be taken instead of higher-powered drugs with greater side effects? Sometimes doctors default to recommending brand-name pharmaceuticals because of a relationship they have with the manufacturers, so this bias filter should be kept in mind.

While it's a good idea to generally listen to our doctors, it's ultimately our decision how we care for our bodies. At the same time, if we don't do it, no one else will.

Medication evaluation (mental health). If we're comfortable having conversations about depression, anxiety and other mental health topics with our primary physician, this is the easiest place to start. For many of my clients, there's little reason to involve a specialist when they already have a relationship with a trusted physician.[1]

We can be honest with our primary doctor about what we're experiencing. Even if he's a member of our church, we can choose to trust him as a professional under ethical obligation to protect our privacy. If not, we need another doctor anyway. Does he feel confident treating our symptoms, or would we be better off working with a psychiatrist? A lack of confidence on either side means a specialist referral would be best.

Ben wasn't dealing with clinical depression, only symptoms from his low testosterone and vitamin D deficiency that mimicked depression. In addition to his medication changes, his doctor gave him a few other suggestions alongside the behavioral changes we made in our coaching together. All of it worked together to strengthen his overall physical health.

By the way, asking for help from a medical professional isn't a sign of spiritual weakness; it's just taking care of our bodies in a fallen world.

Nutrition plan. I'm not advocating a diet here, but modifying our eating habits to be healthier in a way that's sustainable over time. Ben eliminated a few of his "go to" fast food joints altogether, while others he limited to no more than twice weekly. He also swapped his favorite kettle corn chips for baked sweet potato chips and eliminated ice cream from his grocery list altogether.

Other clients have reduced their caloric intake by 20 percent, cut their second helpings by half or gradually increased their water intake toward a target of one half-ounce per pound of body weight.

Whatever our current eating habits are, the idea is to simply start there, taking one or two action steps for improvement at a time until they can be sustained for thirty days. Then picking another while holding on to the one we've already modified.

Ben came to discover that certain emotional states were motivating his sweets craving. His out-of-nowhere hankering for boxed snacks and sweets was a convenient disguise that masked his emotional feelings of loneliness and stress. In some ways, they served a similar coping function to his pornography.

Sleep plan. Back in his college days, Ben used to stay up late finishing last-minute projects, only to run late for his first class the next morning. Trained by his collegiate days, he still averaged less than six hours of sleep, assuming he didn't surf for porn trying to fall asleep the night before.

With an Internet filter and an accountability buddy in place, Ben then learned to discipline his video games so he could more consistently get in bed by 11 p.m. This increased his sleep to at least seven hours nightly. Giving up these more selfish late-night activities also helped him realize he was taking steps to prepare himself for future family life as well.

Matt (the nonprofit director) used to read in bed prior to falling asleep. He learned to fall asleep faster by putting a chair in his bedroom and reading while sitting in his new chair. This way, his getting into bed triggered his brain for sleeping rather than reading time. It can be helpful to create a sleep routine (such as reading or praying in a bedroom chair) just before bedtime. If possible, we should keep stressful stuff out of our bedroom, such as paying bills, difficult marital discussions and office work. These are necessary of course, just not in the bedroom.

James (the Christian speaker) experienced a faster onset of sleep by practicing a few ideas for destressing from *Stress Management for Dummies*, such as hanging thick curtains on his bedroom windows and keeping a memo pad on his nightstand to let go of any "to do" items that hit his brain while he was trying to fall asleep.[2]

The more we understand sleep, the more we realize how important it is. Sleep gives our bodies an ability to restore everything depleted from the previous day. Even mild sleep deprivation over time can result in symptoms of diabetes, hypertension, obesity, depression and other conditions.

Exercise plan. The best exercise plan is the one we'll actually carry out on a regular basis. Ben enjoyed playing racquetball periodically with a few of his coworkers. However, he decided to ask one of them to commit to playing twice weekly. He eventually added a Nautilus workout at the gym two other days per week.

For men with young kids in the home (like me), this may not be realistic at all. Actually, I have a sheet of "quick easy workplace workouts," which is a list of exercises that can be done using my desk and other office furniture.[3] It's about the best I get during this difficult season of child rearing. The key is finding something doable for our season of life and on our family budget. The point isn't "getting it right," but taking a step toward improvement—even if our starting point currently is no exercise at all.

Stress reduction/relaxation. This could be as simple as paying focused attention to our breathing in and breathing out rhythmically. Or, something more regimented, such as the following: Sit upright in a chair, close your eyes, and follow this pattern—inhale through your nose for three seconds, hold your breath for twelve seconds, exhale through your mouth for six seconds. Repeat six times, with a more "explosive" exhale at the very end, allowing your breathing to slowly return to normal before getting out of the chair and moving on with your day.

These breathing exercises are simple and easy to do and generally result in most people feeling less distracted and more relaxed. They can also help facilitate a subtle adjustment in the pH balance of our bodies, which produces a calming effect.

Reading a book on stress reduction, spending fifteen minutes listening to classical or "easy listening" music, taking a ten-minute power nap, buying a massage chair—it might take some experimentation, but finding an effective method to increase relaxation and reduce stress can be a great investment in our overall mental health and productivity.

Sexual education. Like most men, Ben didn't recall any helpful sex education from his parents growing up other than, "There's a book over there, Son. If you got questions, check it out." "At least my dad didn't give me a *Playboy*!" Ben joked. Another client's sex education from his parents wasn't any better. His mom's parting words going out the door with friends was often, "Just keep it in your pants, Son."

There's a good reason many of us grew up without much of a clue, relying on little else beyond lore of middle-school locker rooms and our own adolescent experimentation.

Ben's feelings about his anatomy affect his view of himself more than they will his future bride's actual physical satisfaction. She'll likely be more focused on relational connecting in sex and, where orgasm is a concern, length won't likely interfere due to a woman's sexual stimulation being derived more from the outer parts of her body than those deep inside her.

But like Ben, we won't know that unless we're willing to find good, healthy books on sexuality from a Christian worldview. Pornography reinforces our sexual inadequacy and perpetuates lies, such as the lie that all women have testosterone-driven sex drives.

REMEMBER, WE'RE ON A GRACE-BASED PATH

"God, grant me the serenity to accept the things I cannot change, courage to change the things I can, and the wisdom to know the difference." These well-known words from Reinhold Niebuhr's Serenity Prayer are a grace-based reminder that some things about our bodies we can improve; others, we cannot. We can accept our bodies as they are, and not as we would have them, allowing God to use our uniqueness (especially the unchangeable parts) to his glory.

We must also acknowledge the trade-offs involved in pursuing greater discipline in our physical health. In the real world, we can't maximize all the areas for improvement mentioned here. If we have to sacrifice improving one area and instead prioritize another, so be it. Taking responsibility for what we can in our current season of life is yet another example of a grace-based approach to walking the path.

Keep in mind, these are all areas that *can* be problematic. Every person is different. If we find more than one or two areas needing attention, we don't have to be overwhelmed. Grace to self is more focused on progress than arrival.

The bottom line is that we don't need to be told all the areas for improvement with regard to our bodies. We know them. More than likely, what we need more is permission to pick one small area of change to implement over the next thirty days. *Just one.* It can be small: eliminate one food item from our diet, give up one TV show to bed down thirty minutes earlier, lace up our shoes and walk the neighborhood for just five minutes twice a week.

Any positive change can—and should—be celebrated. Sharing our intentions with someone else allows them to celebrate and encourage our incremental progress. Then we can pick another small area for change and put it into practice over the next thirty days, while keeping in place our previous gains. It's not rocket science. It's sanctification (Phil 2:12-13).

But what if we find ourselves in that 70 percent of Christian leaders who have no one they call a close friend? That's a missing link for many of us, and it's a topic deserving of its own consideration.

9

THE DISCIPLINE OF
INTIMATE RELATIONSHIPS

*Two people are better off than one, for they can help each other
succeed. If one person falls, the other can reach out and help.
But someone who falls alone is in real trouble.*

Ecclesiastes 4:9-10 nlt

*A friend is someone who knows the song in your heart and
can sing it back to you when you have forgotten the words.*

Unknown

■■✝■■

While inimate relationships are difficult for men in general, they're
especially challenging for those in Christian leadership. In addition to the reasons previously mentioned (being at the top,
standing in for God and being celebrated), we often feel as if we're
in perpetual competition with other men. Being in Christian leadership doesn't change the essence of that struggle. We merely place a
veneer of spirituality over the top of it by talking about growth,
reach, baptisms, our personal brand and other lingo. These aren't
wrong, per se. It's just that competition in ministry leads us to

protect ourselves from being vulnerable and known intimately—
the very things most needed for healthy relationships to work.

I've already alluded to the importance of intimate relationships.
It's been peppered throughout the previous chapters in my encouragement to speak honestly with those we can trust and risk being
known in the place of our deepest needs. But before accepting the
myth that men don't need relationships as much as women do, remember that God himself experiences relationship among the
persons of the Trinity. If we're created in his image, this seems in-
dicative of a deep relational need for us men, too.

Clearly, there are unique challenges here for the Christian leader.
But challenges don't give us a free pass on an intrinsic human need.
If we're to flourish in our ministry calling, we've simply got to figure
this one out.

WALKING OUT RELATIONAL DISCIPLINE

Here are some of the main types of intimate relationships we'll
want to consider for working toward relational wholeness and
health, starting with foundational relationships and moving to
more specialized options for those who might need more focused
attention in this area.

Same-gendered friendships. Relationship is at the foundation of
what God meant when he said about Adam, "It is not good that the
man should be alone" (Gen 2:18). Yes, this reference is traditionally
applied to marriage at nearly every wedding, and this is most certainly
true. However, the passage has a more obvious and basic application
when taken simply as it's stated—it's not good for any human to be
alone. If even God isn't alone, then we shouldn't be either.

By the way, to whom was God making this comment? It wasn't
directed to Adam, and no other humans had yet been created. This
comment was expressed in the context of God's relationship among

the persons of the Trinity—further evidence of the relational nature of the Godhead, with clear implications for us created in his image.

While our marriage is arguably the most important human relationship, the most *basic* of human relationships is the one existing between same-gendered friends. They are most like us and, therefore, have the greatest ability to speak into our lives from a similar perspective. For married men, these relationships can also encourage us to be the best husbands we can be to our wives. Such men can often speak into our lives in ways our wives can't. And to be honest, if our wives offered direct advice on how to be a better husband, there's a real chance our fragile male egos might not receive it well, anyway.

Married and unmarried alike need relationships with other men who can understand and encourage them. The trick as Christian leaders, of course, is not only finding such friendships but also risking the pursuit of them. (Senior pastor Brad Hoffmann and I devote considerable attention to this problem and suggest practical steps toward developing deep friendships in our book, *Preventing Ministry Failure*.[1])

This is where we must refuse to be part of the 70 percent of Christian male leaders without a close friend. Yes, it's unfamiliar and perhaps even scary. From my vantage point, given all the carnage I've witnessed for more than a decade, it's the most neglected of all relationships among men who are Christian leaders. On the other hand, the most successful cases I work with are the ones who are willing to leverage male friendships—either by deepening ones they already have or by forging new ones.

Daniel primarily pursued male friendships within the context of his Twelve-Step communities; Matt and James did the same. Ben and Tim decided to take a few existing friendships and take the intentional risk, over time, to share at the level of their deepest needs.

Periodically I work with Christian leaders who, because of the risks, have no intention of telling anyone about their struggles other than me. There's generally a direct relationship between such men and the prominence and visibility of their leadership. I get it. Yes, we can lose it all if we share with another man at this level of vulnerability. But I've not really seen a great track record of recovery when we choose to "go it alone with God." Like the rich young ruler, we sometimes have to be willing to lay it all on the line to follow Jesus.

Tim (the worship leader with bidirectional attractions) started on the path by contacting me for help. With a bit of strong encouragement over our first two months together, he reluctantly joined a support community near his home. Within the next few months, Tim found a new freedom in his ability to share a more honest picture of his real life with the men in his group. As he continued pursuing sexual integrity, Tim intentionally risked reconnecting with an old friend he felt safe to share the details of his new path. This went well and redeemed an old buddy into a close friend and confidant—a true brother.

Tim is an example of what a willingness to surrender pride and risk reaching out looks like. It's sometimes nothing short of amazing to see what God can do when we're willing to risk like that. Here's the bottom line: wherever we find ourselves along the path of improving our sexual integrity, we'll benefit most from accepting the risks associated with letting others into our world as opposed to the risks of staying in the shadows all alone.

Spouse. For those of us who are married, the closest relationship we should have in this life to another person is with our wife. The Bible not only speaks of two becoming "one" in marriage, but also of marriage as a living representation of our relationship with Jesus (Eph 5:25-27). Remember the passage in Hebrews 4:16 about Jesus being our helper in time of need? This same word *helper* is used when the Old Testament refers to our wives as "helpers" (Gen 2:24). A physician is a literal lifesaver, and this is the same metaphor Scripture uses for the role God intends our wives to play for us married guys.

I confess that I didn't understand this truth early in my marriage, which was evidence of my own spiritual and relational immaturity. I'm increasingly realizing the vital role my wife plays in helping me grow into a mature Christian man, husband and leader.

I'll admit, however, that just about every step I've taken to allow her into my intimate world during the course of our marriage has felt risky to me. I still choose to do it, so obviously I perceive it to be highly valuable. And while it doesn't feel as risky as it once did, it still challenges me. But when I take a risk and see it bear fruit, I'm encouraged to risk it all the more. Faith in her is a lot like faith in God. When my risk is rewarded, I'm encouraged to do it all the more.

Of course, my wife isn't perfect, so I have to give her grace sometimes, too. But that's not hard to do, given how messed up I can be sometimes and how my choices sometimes negatively affect her.

There are two ways to improve our personal intimacy with our wives. One is simply to take the risk with her directly. Each time we do, we learn how to do it better next time. Risks would include sharing our positive and negative emotions, fears and dreams, and sin struggles, both past and present. Yes, to do this squarely places us at risk for losing them based upon their response. But this risk is the only way to fully redeem our marriage as the safe haven we always hoped it would be.

The other way is to discuss this topic in the context of another relationship mentioned in this chapter. Relationships outside our marriage can give us objective input, serving as incubators for encouraging greater intimacy with our wives over time.

Mentor. In the early days of American academia, a mentoring model existed in higher education. Back then, mentoring was seamlessly integrated into the general training of a young man into mature adulthood.

Nowadays, such relationships seem few and far between unless they're intentionally sought out by the one desiring mentoring. I would love to see a greater emphasis on mentoring among Christian leaders who are willing to proactively raise up younger leaders. I appreciate folks like Bobb Biehl who've tirelessly championed mentoring for decades.[2]

As it stands, a younger leader who wants mentoring from a seasoned veteran is, for the most part, required to proactively pursue such a mentor. Engaging some basic reading on the subject can help us cast a clear vision for what we want from a potential mentor.

A word to the wise: we may have to ask multiple men before finding one willing to walk with us over the long haul. But on the other side of a few rejections just might be someone who can really pour into us.

While Ben (the never-married leader) had such a relationship with his boss at work, his boss knew nothing about Ben's deepest area of shame and struggle. This significantly hamstrung Ben's ability to receive the most beneficial parts of the relationship. So there are downsides to developing a mentoring relationship with someone who also supervises us in a work setting.

By contrast, I knew an associate pastor who, after his emotional affair and two-year formal restoration process, was hired by a church in full knowledge of his story. The church had a history of participating in pastoral restoration. In effect, the senior pastor of his new church embraced the informal role of mentor in his life. Knowing his full story made this possible.

Whether a workmate or supervisor can effectively serve as a

mentor takes discernment and prayer. Just don't discount it out of hand, as each case is unique.

Spiritual director. While very common in some denominations, seeking spiritual direction is completely uncharted territory for others. Spiritual directors are part mentors, part coaches and part pastors. A spiritual director is essentially someone trained to help others personally walk in step with the Spirit—the true Spiritual Director of the believer.

If engaged in a more official capacity, the spiritual director preserves more objectivity and can give more objective feedback in his or her spiritual direction, like the role of a coach. However, some spiritual directors are more informal and familial with those they help and function more with the feel of a mentor or mature spiritual friend. Emphasis is on application and walking out spiritual principles in the various aspects and relationships of one's life. For men willing to be guided in this way, spiritual direction can be a valuable part of taking off the leader mask and walking out a more personal walk with Jesus.

For the past few years, I've led telephone-based groups for men pursuing sexual integrity as a part of their "phase two" recovery process. Once men have spent sufficient focus on sobriety from sexual behaviors, the focus in recovery shifts toward overall life serenity. Instead of asking questions such as, "How can I stop acting out?" we focus more on questions such as, "How do I engage spiritual warfare, sanctification and biblical masculinity *in light of* my sexual integrity recovery?" In essence, these groups are focused more on men's spiritual formation.

Professional counselor/coach. Christian leaders can benefit from working with a professional specifically trained to provide targeted help, especially if that professional has experience working with sexual integrity issues or with the unique population of

Christian leaders. State-licensed professional counselors or certified coaches (such as board certified coach or master/professional
certified coach) can offer objective, specialized support addressing
key areas of concern.

Generally, professional counselors offer a more reparative function
related to psychological trauma, clinical depression/anxiety, emotional dysfunction and mental illness, such as bipolar disorder. Professional coaches are skilled at helping leaders productively move
from where they are (a generally healthy but dissatisfied place) to
where they ultimately want to be. A few of us who were trained as
counselors and now function as coaches are able to do effective
coaching work while offering knowledgeable referrals for those
needing additional levels of support.[3]

Deciding between a counselor or coach isn't always an either/or
proposition, as it's also possible to engage counseling for mental
health management while still starting the journey with a specialized
coach like me for sexual integrity recovery. Each man's story is
unique and so is each man's process for engaging the path. The important thing is to start one side or the other (counselor or coach)
and ask the first professional engaged to help you more objectively
determine if other professionals need to be on your team in the
current season.

Tim engaged my services from early on in his sexual integrity
recovery journey. As I mentioned earlier, it took about a month to
convince him to take the risk of attending support environments,
the same one he's now been attending for years. We initially began
working together weekly, reducing his frequency over time to every
other week and now to once monthly. The frequency and duration
of a professional one-on-one service is unique for each leader, depending on the level of support desired. For Tim, our early times
together centered around creating a strong recovery plan as well as

helping him make a full disclosure of his past and current sexual struggles with his wife. In time, our focus shifted from sobriety regarding masturbation to the pursuit of serenity and overall health in all his relationships.

Too often, I and my like-minded colleagues end up serving as the last ditch option for Christian leaders in need of recovery. This often occurs on the other side of some discovery of their moral failure. And I get it. It's an easier "sell" to acknowledge the need for such help after the fall and not so easy before.

While some may not have difficulty engaging a professional counselor or coach, others go to seemingly great lengths to do so. I've had clients make up reasons to secretarial staff and spouses about the exact nature of our interactions. Like Nicodemus, they come under the cloak of night in terms of the challenges they navigate just to get to me without being found out. But I suppose I'd rather this be the case than the continued lying just to keep living a double life.

Regardless, if this level of help is needed, it's worth whatever it takes to have a professional skilled at helping in this area. While I can help at any point along a leader's journey, I'm generally more effective the earlier I can become a part of the team. This is true for both personal recovery and personal loss. More power exists to save marriages and ministries when prevention and disclosure are our tools rather than having to deal with the damage in the wake of post-discovery.

DEEPER INTERVENTION

Numerous Christian ministries are dedicated to helping ministers thrive. Such ministries range from Barnabas-type encouragement to consultation to pastoral counseling/coaching to reduced-cost getaways and structured respite time for ministry leaders. The costs

vary from full fee to free and all points in between. Focus on the
Family and CareGivers Forum are two examples that maintain comprehensive lists of such ministries (see appendix C).

But Christian leaders on the verge of burnout or moral failure in
ministry need a more intensive resource than a quiet getaway from
the noise of life. This was the case for Matt, who was so distraught
over a fellow employee opening one of his "special" packages that
he plunged into a major bout of depression. Prior to my time
working with him, he attended a residential program for sexual
addiction recovery.

Intensive/residential programs run anywhere from days to
months in duration. Some have built-in psychiatry for those who
need such support. They can be a bit pricy, but financial assistance
can sometimes be accessed through the program directly or from
concerned loved ones within our families or the ministries with
which we're affiliated. Leaders being terminated can sometimes have
the cost of such programs written into their severance agreement.[4]

Specialized support groups. For those contending with life-dominating issues, compulsions and addictions, specialized support
groups such as Celebrate Recovery (distinctly Christian) or Sexaholics
Anonymous (loosely religious) can be tremendously beneficial or even
necessary for added support, especially in the early stages of recovery.

Some leaders may have an initial negative reaction to the idea
of participating in such groups out of concern for confidentiality.
Sure, that risk does exist. But keep in mind that being "outed" by
another participant requires that person to out themselves in
order to share their knowledge of our being a participant. So, this
risk is somewhat self-mitigating.

Regardless, some leaders come to realize that their lives are a
subtle ticking time bomb anyway, support group or not. For these,
risking exposure in getting help to avert a catastrophe is preferred

to continuing Russian roulette and eventually hitting the proverbial loaded chamber.

Virtual support groups also exist, such as the phone-based groups through XXXchurch.com.[5] These are especially beneficial for those leaders who aren't ready to reach out to other forms of support.

For Tim, becoming a part of a weekly support environment provided more freedom and encouragement than he ever thought possible. Tim had real misgivings about taking the step early on, and it took more than a month to convince him to do so. But within a few weeks, his fear gave way to a familiarity with other men in the group and he began taking small steps to share bits of his reasons for being there.

At first, he shared more generally about struggling with sexual integrity. A few weeks after that, he took more risk by talking about his struggle with fantasy and masturbation, as well as his overall marital difficulties. It took a few months, however, for him to finally own the deepest shame of his same-sex attractions. With each microdisclosure, Tim received more encouragement from other participants. His openness seemed to encourage others' willingness toward greater transparency as well.

EXHALE

Certainly all of us have improvements we could make to boost our overall health. Some, of course, have more room for improvement than others. If some of us have farther to go, it's likely because we've been on an unhealthy road for longer than others. As I once heard pastor Charles Stanley say, "It's the law of the harvest: we reap what we sow, more than we sow and later than we sow."

So true.

Nevertheless, our direction on the path is the same, as is our overall stride: one decision and one improvement at a time. So let's have a grace-based conversation about taking that next step.

10

PURSUING THE PATH OF HOPE

A person who is full refuses honey,
but even bitter food tastes sweet to the hungry.

Proverbs 27:7 nlt

Ain't a soul on this entire earth ain't got a burden
to carry he don't understand, you ain't alone in that. . . .
But you been carryin' this one long enough . . .
Time to go on . . . lay it down . . .

Bagger Vance to Rannulph Junah,
The Legend of Bagger Vance

For God has not given us a spirit of fear,
but of power and of love and of a sound mind.

2 Timothy 1:7 nkjv

■■✝■■

When we see someone who has experienced a big fall from ministry or someone who's suffering consequences from their poor choices, it's helpful to consider how they started walking such a destructive road in the first place.

Often, it starts with a single choice that (eventually) leads to negative consequences. That leads to other consequential choices in an effort to live with the pain from the original choice. The load only becomes heavier from trying to hold it all together on their own. While others may not see it on the outside, the internal stress from living with compounding consequences is burdensome. The negative cycle feeds on itself.

It's similar to a young couple who begins using credit cards to cover monthly expenses rather than adjusting their lifestyle. With each passing month, interest, fees and penalties increasingly add to their load of debt. Paying the minimum payment each month can keep a couple stuck for decades and eventually lead to bankruptcy.

But as everyone knows, the way to get out of debt is one small decision at a time. They could start by paying off the smallest one first, paying off the highest interest card, taking a part-time job or radically cutting their grocery budget. Any and all of the strategies will work. As the debt decreases, so do interest, fees and penalties.

At some point, they reach a tipping point: no debt. Beyond this, every dollar saved becomes a servant to their purpose of living debt free. A dollar could serve them in an emergency savings fund, invested with interest, invested in a retirement account or used to fund the down payment of a new business venture. Just as each dollar of debt fed on itself with even greater debt, each dollar of saving accomplishes the opposite, organically producing more savings and greater financial freedom.

Small changes made persistently over time slowly get the young couple out of debt. Time is their ally, and there's no magic bullet. Only a fool would recommend that they play the lottery to solve the problem.

So it is with the journey of sanctification toward greater sexual integrity. There's no magic prayer to serve as a lottery ticket for us to win the prize of no longer struggling with sexual temptation. Our journey is about becoming more maturely conformed to Christ. It's less about deliverance and more about growing up to live within our means. That's because our sexuality isn't an evil to banish but a gift we must learn to steward well as his image bearers. That gift is a reflection of God's own image. Our job is to learn to harness its power for the good our Creator intended.

LOOKING BACK

We're all in different places on this journey. Some have a lot of re-covery work to do; others simply need to learn a few better methods for healthy self-care and reflecting kingdom values in our walk. Yet each of us can take steps to become healthier and, consequently, travel further down the road in our experience of sexual integrity.

The place to start is admission of our need to surrender to the path in the first place. Laying down our pride allows us to pick up humility and receive God's grace. We put active safeguards in place for no longer returning to our old ways of sexual sin. We also begin recognizing our need for quicker and earlier surrender to God when we face future temptations. Remember, this is a sanctification skill we develop with each opportunity we have to practice it.

We then consider our need for improved discipline in becoming more emotionally aware, personalizing our journey with God, caring well for our physical bodies and leveraging a few intimate relationships in pursuit of real community. These help ensure our overall health and move us in the direction of more satisfaction with the good things God has for us. It strengthens our ability to say in the face of temptation, "No thanks, I'm full."

MOVING FORWARD

No matter how much we find ourselves in debt with regard to sexual integrity, it's time we do something more about it. Whether heavily in debt, somewhat in debt or debt free but with little savings for buffering future challenges, greater freedom promotes greater flourishing in our Christian lives, our calling and our ability to encourage other Christian leaders onto the same path.[1]

Would we shame a young couple needing financial counseling for thousands of dollars in credit card debt? Of course not. They need a plan for not feeling overwhelmed and encouragement for taking one step at a time toward financial freedom. Likewise, we will also benefit from a grace-based approach, just like the one we would extend to the young couple in financial straits. So let's cast a vision and create a plan for a sexual integrity path—one that's filled with hope.

Depending on our situation, we might feel overwhelmed by the number of areas in which improvement needs to occur. Big and small, these areas are often interconnected. Feelings of sadness impact our perception of how God feels toward us. Our difficulty in perceiving God's unconditional acceptance spills over into a lack of confidence to pursue or trust friendships. Marital discord leads to overeating or loss of sleep afterwards. Overindulgence on yesterday's pizza causes sluggishness and struggle with mental focus the next morning.

It can feel like a tangled spider web at times.

But what if bad news were actually good news in disguise? If everything's interconnected, each impacting the others in some way, then making a simple decision to start *anywhere* would reverse the downward spiral. Like paying down debt or increasing cash reserve, what if every choice we make that's consistent with our values strengthens our ability to do it again and again?

THE JUNGLE PATH: A SANCTIFICATION PARABLE

Imagine that we traveled by helicopter to a remote location some-where deep in the jungle. There's a well-worn, eight-mile winding path that can get us from that point to the nearest village in about an hour. But as the village is only three miles away as the crow flies, we could get there much faster if we could cut a new path through the dense jungle.

If we were only given a machete for cutting the new path, how long would it take to hack our way to arrive at the village? Whatever the answer is, it's much longer than an hour, guaranteed! There's no telling how many times we'd have to stop and restart because of exhaustion. And since we're trying to get there as quickly as possible, we'd only be hacking enough overgrowth to squeeze our body through to take the next step, where we'd have to do it all over again. Literally, ad nauseum.

So, let's say it takes eight hours. The next day, we're dropped by helicopter and asked to do it all over again. On day two, we don't have to hack quite as vigorously, but there'd still be plenty of work to do. Again, we'd only do as much as needed to get through. This time, hacking through only takes seven hours.

Day three is more of the same, only taking six hours. Day four, less than six hours. You get the idea. Each successive trip takes less time because we're building on our efforts from the previous day.

What if on day five, we decided, "Forget it! This is too much work! Let's take the old path today." We could do that, right? On day six, if we come to our senses and decide it's worth the effort to continue cutting the new road, are we back to an eight-hour hackfest? Of course not. Sure, there's been one day's worth of regrowth yesterday because we decided not to travel the new path. But it's only *one* day's growth. While it'll take a bit longer to ac-complish our ultimate task of creating a shorter pathway, we can start again without giving up most of our previous gains.

By the way, what's happening to the old path every day we're not taking it? Ever so slowly, it's becoming overgrown. As we continue to daily cut a new path, it's becoming easier, while the old path is slowly becoming overgrown from lack of use.

Eventually we'll reach a tipping point, where the new path takes just as long to travel as the old, winding path. If we persist beyond this point, something interesting happens. The new path actually takes less time to travel than the old one. At this tipping point, the new path becomes the easier path—the new path of least resistance.[2]

TEMPTATION-RESISTANT TRANSFORMATION IN REAL TIME

On day one, the idea that the new path would ever become the path of least resistance is difficult, if not impossible, to envision. But it's a simple application of all human behavior change: small changes at a time, sustained over time, lead to real transformation. When sustained beyond the tipping point, it leads to *temptation-resistant* transformation.

Notice I didn't say *temptation-proof* transformation. That won't happen this side of heaven, I'm afraid. But that's okay. Participation with God in our sanctification is real change, and that's better any day over staying miserably stuck.

If we had a migraine headache that registered a 9.5 out of 10, would we really scoff at an intervention that reduces it to a 5 or 6? Sure, we'd much prefer to have the headache gone. But anything we can do to make it more manageable empowers us to not live distracted by the migraine. Similarly, anything we can do to become more resistant to sexual temptation empowers us to more effectively live out our God-honoring values and more easily ignore temptations and impulses.

So, here's what the journey looks like played out in real time. Today, we read through appendix A and create our own personalized checklist of areas important for our own integrity path, selecting one or two areas for improvement over the next short season.

Tomorrow or next week, something triggers our sexual appetite and tempts us to veer off the path. What do we do? First, we pray a prayer of surrender to the Lord. We ask God for his strength in our weakness. Second, we fully embrace God's grace the moment we surrender. In a perfect world, we would realize the temptation at the initial moment of impact. However, regardless how quickly or slowly we surrender, we can ask for his direction about practical next steps. Third, we listen and wait, trusting the Holy Spirit to bring to mind any practical steps that are needed. Confess to an accountability buddy? Jog the neighborhood? Spend five or ten minutes in prayer? Write in our new journal? None of these answers is better than another, unless the Spirit prompts us otherwise. If God isn't clear about the very next step, we can trust they're all connected and that each encourages and energizes the others. Once these steps have been taken, we celebrate any victories (no matter how small) and learn from our mistakes.

This is the essence of a grace-based approach to sexual integrity recovery. We're not winking at sin; we're partnering with God in a sanctification path that is being perfected until we reach the finish line or until the day God brings the finish line to us.

WHERE THEY ARE NOW

The stories shared in this book were inspired by the lives of real men I've had the privilege of walking alongside for a portion of their integrity recovery journey. We know what started them on the path and we've watched some of the steps they took in our work together. But how are they now?

Daniel is still in relationship with both his wife and his ministry. No one outside of the couple ever knew of his challenges, except for a few couples closest to them and the men in his support group environment (that's not to say his marriage has been without its share of challenges). As a couple in recovery, they participated for over a year in marriage counseling to weather the storm. Years later, Daniel still thrives in part due to his regular Twelve-Step attendance. We still touch base monthly for maintenance coaching, though we've long since transitioned into general coaching from intense focus on sobriety-related issues. He's been sober from alcohol and sexual infidelity for years.

Matt lost his nonprofit ministry position at the initial point of discovery. It took him months to unpack his entire story, which was in part during his residential program and continued into his initial months of follow-up coaching after that. In time, he gave a complete disclosure to his wife, who maintained a strong commitment to stay in the marriage throughout the process and is still with him today. It took Matt well over a year to gain traction in long-term sobriety from pornography and masturbation. He still struggles with sexual temptations, although not to the degree he once did. There also has been occasional reengagement of both behaviors. However, Matt's responses are different now. He's maintaining his commitment to confess to his wife and accountability buddy within twenty-four hours. This has helped rebuild trust with Ashley. It has also increased his confidence to understand his deeper emotional impulses and redirect them toward healthier choices. Matt was recently reemployed in a different ministry context, and now has a supervisor who's not only in full knowledge of his past but also an active part of his accountability team.

James lost his pastoral position and has now found secular employment that's sufficient to provide for his family. He still grieves the loss of serving in ministry, but he's also very grateful for the experience because it has transformed his marriage. Both he and his wife required years of strong support from professionals and separate support group environments. But the investment paid off. James reports an intimacy with his wife (both emotional and sexual) that's far beyond his prior experience. His relationship with God is revitalized and more personally satisfying than ever.

Ben is still unmarried and remains in ministry. He has gained insight into his reasons for being pulled toward pornography and has experienced significant improvement in his ability to resist. Ben has chosen not to share his struggle with his boss for fear of being terminated. He's also been resistant to attending a support group for fear of word getting back to his boss. While maintaining his boss as his "professional hat" mentor, he did recently risk asking another older Christian leader about serving as more of a "spiritual director" mentor. He was thrilled when the man agreed. While Ben does have one friend who knows his full story, he doesn't maintain regular contact and his accountability with him is limited. This remains an area for improvement moving forward. He maintains regular contact in coaching and has made strides with regard to the care of his body, including increased energy due to his coordinated medical treatment with his doctor. He still looks forward to being married and maintains a commitment that his future wife will know all the relevant details about his sexual history. His story is still unfolding.

Tim remains in ministry, but his marriage took years to rebuild. After a time of separation, he and Jillian have reunited and have been together ever since—although their sexual relationship has only recently returned, both due to her rebuilding trust and his rebuilding confidence to pursue her sexually. He's still fearful, but works diligently on his thought life to see himself as God sees him with regard to his sexual identity. Tim maintains attendance in a recovery environment and has a close buddy who is the strongest encourager of both Tim and his marriage. Tim reports being more open to sharing things in his recovery group. He's also learning greater proactivity in sharing his emotional self with Jillian and is encouraged in the direction of his marriage.

A BIGGER VISION OF HOPE

These stories may or may not reflect your own. You might say, "That's not me" as you read these accounts.

They're not me, either. But then again, they are. As Bonhoeffer once wrote, "If my sinfulness appears to be in any way smaller or less detestable in comparison with the sins of others, I am still not recognizing my sinfulness at all."[3] Their stories still resonate with me in that their road to sexual integrity recovery is the very same one I'm traveling.

That's the message of hope. No matter where our lives have taken us, the Christian leaders' path to sexual integrity is a path big enough for all of us to walk together. And we're better off if we take the journey together. This is the essence of Christian community, even for those in leadership. Perhaps especially for those in leadership. The rubber meets the road where we meet one another and walk together, doing *real* life together, especially related to the most intimate areas of our lives.

The pathway to sexual integrity is a path of sanctification, not perfection. It's a path that starts with our willingness to surrender to the Lord, followed by a humble willingness to engage the journey in full awareness of our emotions, spirits and bodies, and in relationship with a few others who really know us and are committed to walking alongside us as we travel an imperfect path.

We don't have to go it alone anymore. Risk reaching out to *one person* who might walk with you as you take the next few steps. If you don't know who that man might be, keep asking the Lord to give you direction until he provides at least one other man to walk with you. Be patient. It's worth it.

If I can help, reach out to me. If you're more motivated to reach out to somebody else, then by all means do that. The actual next few steps you choose to take (beyond surrender to the path) aren't all that important. What's important is that you take one. Then another one.

> Take another step, take another step
> When the road ahead is dark
> And you don't know where to go
> Take another step, take another step
> Trust God and take another step.[4]

SERENITY: A VISION BEYOND SOBRIETY

God longs to give us a bigger vision for our lives and ministries, one that's far beyond our preoccupations or periodic struggles with sexual distractions.

When I first start working with someone, our focus is almost always on sobriety. That is, it's on stopping the life-draining behaviors. It'll get us started, but that motivation isn't going to sustain over the long haul. Let's take a look at just some of the more tangible big-picture motivators for being on this path over time.

Freedom from the guilt of being caught or the consequences of future poor choices. When we're in the middle of it, we often don't realize the burden we bear from our sin struggle. It's only when we gain some distance from it that we realize the weight we were carrying. The unburdened life under Jesus' yoke is very different than the burden of our sin struggle. A life free of secrets withheld from our most intimate relationships encourages us to remain on the path.

Less preoccupation with sexual temptation. The more we practice the principles of recovery, the greater the confidence we have to continue doing so and to more quickly return to the path when we stray. It doesn't prevent us from making mistakes; but it does give us the confidence to know how to more quickly recognize when we've strayed and more quickly return to the path. This discipline also trains us to recognize detours ahead of choosing them, resulting in increased confidence to not choose them in the future.

Greater respect from our wives. When they see something different about path we're now on, they'll have more respect for us. This will also help them to develop a growing confidence in their ability to trust us moving forward. We can't force their trust, but we *can* become more trustworthy men. It will be up to them to choose to trust us, but they can't make us more trustworthy. That's our job.

Increased support through close relationships with men who really know us. The benefits of this countercultural path among Christian leaders is difficult to overestimate. The synergy that comes from having a few men who really know us, warts and all, is tremendous. In addition, living openly among these relationships circumvents shame and steals a significant tool the enemy so often uses to torpedo Christian leaders.

Stronger confidence in our ministry calling. This "being known" approach to life and ministry can lead to dramatic results. What would life be like if we had no fear from guilt, shame and the possible consequences from our sin? What if we had genuine respect from our wives and a few close Christian brothers who really knew us? Such freedom can result in a greater confidence to do the unique things God has called us to do in our marriages, our families and our ministries.

Ability to more boldly speak from the full weight of our true voice. This is where we can truly fulfill our destinies as Christian leaders. Our ability to leave a unique footprint for others to follow is partly dependent on our ability to humbly own our broken path, allowing God to use it much like he did that little boy's loaves and fishes with Jesus.

We can't imagine what God wants to do with our lives if we're willing to let him use our lives, including our brokenness, for his glory. We're not necessarily talking thousands of Twitter followers and people crowding the stage after an altar call. But we can have deep impact on the lives of those people that God puts in our sphere of influence. Whether a few or tens of thousands, God has the ability to do transformative work through us in the lives of others if we're willing first to go through our own transformation. It might be painful for a while, but I've seen God tell some real God stories from our willingness to lay it on the line.

THE JOURNEY BEGINS

So here's the simple message. It doesn't matter where we start. Pick any place. Appendix A is a checklist of all the areas we've covered in the previous few chapters. Consider making a list of those areas you know need improvement. Take each one and break it down into its smallest actionable tasks.

Then, just pick one. Any one will do. Pick the hardest one first or pick the easiest one first. Or, pick the one you're most motivated to do right now. All that matters is that your head hits the pillow tonight having taken one step in the direction of becoming more of a man of sexual integrity. Then, wake up and do it all over again the next day, when his mercy's fresh.

We don't have to become discouraged by the days we're not as effective as we'd like. We can learn from our mistakes and wake up the next morning, keeping in step with the Spirit's leading.

In the grand scheme of things, one day's worth of change isn't much change at all. It's like a single little snowflake on a winter's day. By itself, it will fall to the ground and melt on the coldest of days. But stack one snowflake on top of another on top of another, and we create something different altogether. The most substantial recorded snowfalls all have one thing in common: they were all built one snowflake at a time.

A SIMPLE STEP

Ultimately, we won't be convinced to take such courageous action simply because it's the right thing to do, or because we feel guilty for supporting the sex slave industry. Of course, these are true. Instead, we'll find the motivation because something deep inside us yearns for more. We'll be motivated by grace, not law; by a kindled passion for what's right, rather than merely the call of duty; by a longing to recover our hearts and our greater destiny than sheer obligation.

We don't have to be in this alone. God sees exactly where we are. Our struggles may have been private battles for years or even decades. It doesn't have to stay this way. El Roi—*the God who sees*—sees us right where we are. He has now brought us to this place, this moment of time when we can be honest together about our common struggle. You and I are in this now as brothers.

Depending on where we're starting, the next step toward the light might still be in relative darkness. That's okay. Each successive step builds on the one before it and helps to illumine the next one. That's because every step we take is toward the One who *is* light and will give us clearer vision with every step in his direction.

We don't have to worry about what step #20 may require of us: What do we need to share with our wives? Will we have to confess before the board of directors or in front of the entire denomination? These are questions for the One who's already gone before us.

He doesn't see what we are to become but rather *who we already are in him* (2 Cor 5:21; Eph 2:6-7). We are here in this moment, and he is present with us here, not some theoretical place out there. We can trust him to illumine further steps in time. Sufficient is the light he provides us today for the step right in front of us.

If we step out in faith, we'll find him right there. It's a different kind of courage than we expected, but one with the power to loosen the grip of fear and pride that keeps us in perpetual hiding. As a yielded vessel, we become a catalyst for change in the lives of every man we lead.

By the way, if someday we meet each other somewhere along the path, I look forward to celebrating what the Lord has done and is doing in your integrity journey toward him. As you know, we need all the encouragement we can get.

It's all about the next step. So let's get going.

Appendix A

SEXUAL INTEGRITY ACTION STEPS

We will use these stones to build a memorial.
In the future your children will ask you,
"What do these stones mean?"
Then you can tell them . . .

JOSHUA 4:6-7 NLT

A little thing is only a little thing.
But a lot of little things is a big thing.

UNKNOWN

STONES OF REMEMBRANCE

When we were children and went on a vacation with our family to Disney World or the Grand Canyon, we might have brought back a special toy or keepsake from the trip. When we go on a business trip, we might bring back a memento for our kids, such as an item unique to where we traveled. If we've ever participated in a Walk to Emmaus or Tres Dias, we might bring home a rock or other object from nature to remember one of our walks with the Lord.

These stones and other memorabilia serve to remind us of experiences that were important to us. They also serve as touchstones to tell our story, whether we're telling our children and grand-children, those we lead or other fellow journeymen.

Sometimes, they are simply tools to retell ourselves the bigger story God is writing in us. On the shelf in my office, I have a number of trinkets I've collected over the years: a prayer coin, a holding cross, a broken piece of an alabaster jar, a smooth white stone. Each one not only reminds me of a biblical truth but also of a specific experience from my journey with God. For me, they are stones of remembrance. They're not so much stepping stones as tokens reminding me of my commitment to my faith walk and, perhaps more importantly, God's faithful commitment to me and his redemptive work in my imperfect walk.

BEFORE YOU BEGIN . . .

This list has far more action items than is likely relevant for you right now. But hopefully, it's comprehensive enough to contain a few ideas for your own particular application. While there's no correct order, it's my hope that prayerful consideration reveals which of these "stones" are worthy of picking up along the path. Turn each stone over in your hand, allowing the Holy Spirit to speak to you about how God wants to use it as a tool to conform you to look more like Jesus. Once the stone has accomplished its work, you can lay it down with the others as a way of building a monument, both for your remembrance and as a testimony of what the Lord has done through your obedient surrender to him.

Don't fret over getting it "right." The goal is a journey of perpetual discovery to walk out a more faithful sexual integrity tomorrow than where you are today.

Please resist the urge to judge another man's journey based on what's presented here. If a certain item doesn't apply to you, have a grateful heart to God rather than judge someone else's path (Lk 18:10-14). Stay focused on what God's speaking to you.

1. Before you begin, ask the Holy Spirit to open your eyes to anything having application to your journey.

2. Each list refers back to a particular journeyman in each of the related chapters. If needed, reread how that journeyman applied these provisions to his own path (additional resources can be found in appendix C).

3. Review each provision, placing a check next to items you'd like to do something about. Go with your first impulse. You can always come back later and cross something off your list you decide isn't relevant.

4. Review the items checked, selecting no more than one to three items for focus over the coming thirty days. Remember, there's nothing right or wrong about where to start. Easy or difficult, quick or complex, almost any action item is as good a place to start as another. And any action step engaged or completed is an improvement over inaction.

5. Stay focused on these items until they're completed, at which time you can pick up another one or two from your working list.

6. If you're hesitant to write directly in this book, consider the benefits of writing in a private journal. There, you can keep track of current action items, start and complete dates, as well as any relevant notes and insights the Lord reveals to you along the way.

7. Tangible steps in the direction of a goal can give us a feeling of accomplishment, and that's a good thing. Be encouraged with every item you complete.

Know that you have my full encouragement, not from the bleachers or from the sidelines but as a runner running alongside you. I'm running my race, too. Let's encourage one another to keep our eyes fixed on our Coach who's eagerly waiting for us at the finish line.

SURRENDER STEPS

Daniel (the Christian speaker from p. 21) found these helpful in his initial steps to establish a solid sexual integrity. Embracing any of these is an act of surrender to the Lord, as well as a tangible surrender of our right to continue engaging sexual sin.

☐ *daily pledge*: a regular review of our commitment to the path

☐ *the three circles*: the "target" of red, yellow and green zone behaviors (p. 57)

☐ *boundaries*: practical limits to promote safety and rebuild trust

☐ *software for filtering/monitoring*: for use with computers and other electronic devices

☐ *relapse prevention plan*: a written plan of action steps for integrity

EMOTIONAL STEPS

Matt (the nonprofit director from p. 22) was very disconnected from his emotions at the beginning of his journey, but found these helpful in reconnecting with his true heart. Just as the Bible was never meant to be read disconnected from our emotions, neither did God intend our lives to be lived apart from an intentional emotional connection.

☐ *journaling*: use of a structured or unstructured book, whether one specific to our sexual integrity journey or one integrated into a more comprehensive life journal

□ *feelings feedback*: use of the feelings chart p. 68 to increase our awareness of our dynamic feelings state, whether used alone or within the context of a close relationship for feedback

□ *family-of-origin inventory*: drawing or writing out the picture of our family and the impact they've had on the person we've become

□ *abuse inventory*: recognizing and addressing the impact of harmful past relationships

□ *sexual inventory*: exploring the role of past sexual exposures and experiences on both our forming sexual identity and our eventual sexual choices

□ *triggers inventory*: people, places and things (internal and external) that tempt us to reach out for a sexual object or experience

□ *attentiveness*: gentle reframing from negative shame to positive redirection

□ *shame inventory*: recognizing harmful soul messages from childhood and replacing them with God's truth about ourselves

□ *daily serenity tracking*: tracking tools for improving healthy, godly behaviors that build us up along the sexual integrity sanctification journey.

□ *re-creations list (3 Rs)*: practical steps for promoting rest, recess and renewal

SPIRITUAL STEPS

Although James (the rural pastor from p. 23) was good at helping others practice spiritual disciplines, like many other Christian leaders he had difficulty in his own personal application. Even if we're already doing them, there's often a benefit in prioritizing a season of intentional focus on taking these to a more personal, intimate depth in our walk with the Lord.

- ☐ *personal God time*: intentionally inviting God to speak directly into the vulnerable space of our personal lives, without pre-screening its application to someone else's life

- ☐ *lies inventory*: becoming more aware of the distorted messages we hear (from the world, the flesh and the devil) that we may have used to justify unloving and ungodly actions

- ☐ *theology of suffering*: choosing to see suffering as something God is using to accomplish his purposes for our being made to look more like Jesus

- ☐ *other spiritual "disciplines" (including Scripture memorization and meditation)*: all the disciplines we've taught others to engage, but with intentional focus on our own fresh experience of them

PHYSICAL STEPS

Ben (the never-married minister from p. 23) knew he wasn't caring for his body as well as he could have been. After our initial screening, he realized just how deficient his body stewardship was.

- ☐ *physical and blood work*: annual check-ups, routine screenings and periodic blood work to give ourselves feedback on keeping our body in sustainable performance

- ☐ *medication evaluation (general)*: better understood through physicals, doctors' visits and blood work, as well as through readings in health articles and blogs from reliable sources

- ☐ *medication evaluation (mental health)*: prioritized either through discussions with our primary physician or a referral to a recommended psychiatrist

□ *nutrition plan*: practical ways to eat healthier

□ *sleep plan*: pragmatic improvements for both the quantity and quality of our sleep

□ *exercise plan*: realistic ideas for keeping our muscles, hearts and other vital organs in shape through body movement

□ *stress reduction/relaxation*: simple but effective ways to reduce tension and stress

□ *sexual education*: reliable sources for separating fact from fiction about sex to reduce shame, increase confidence and promote health in our marriages

RELATIONAL STEPS

Tim (the worship leader from p. 24) found relationships a "missing link" in his ability to maintain sobriety and move beyond the shame of his struggling sexual identity. While the more specialized of these aren't necessary for everyone, most of us would do well to take a close look at who else God might want as a part of our own real community and as fellow journeymen.

□ *same-gendered friendships*: men who form our small "band of brothers," who walk beside us knowing our vulnerabilities and weaknesses—supporting and caring about us just the same

□ *spouse*: not just about being married, but risking making our marriage "the safest place on earth"—whether emotionally, spiritually, sexually, relationally or in the full disclosure of the true nature of our sexual integrity struggle

□ *mentor*: a seasoned Christian man who intentionally pours into us

□ *spiritual director*: a professional who helps us focus on our own personal spiritual journey

☐ *professional counselor/coach*: someone professionally trained who's walked alongside others on this journey—especially if none of our other ongoing relationships are "in the know" about our current struggles with sexual integrity

☐ *intensive/residential program*: a structured environment where sexual compulsivity and addiction can be the focus, free from the distractions of our regular stressors and obligations

☐ *specialized support groups*: confidential environment as a safe place to intentionally discuss ways for resisting sexual temptation and promoting integrity while still remaining plugged in to our regular routines

Appendix B

MENTORING AND LEADING
OTHER MEN ALONG THE PATH

What you have heard from me in the presence
of many witnesses entrust to faithful men
who will be able to teach others also.

2 TIMOTHY 2:2

■■✝■■

While ministry can be a very self-sacrificial endeavor, Christian leaders need to model what healthy self-care looks like, spiritually and otherwise. And sexual integrity ought to be near the top of the list of the most critical areas in which healthy modeling matters.

However, before you try to help another man, you'll first want to examine your own life. If you've not yet done so, I suggest you go through the checklist in appendix A, referencing the corresponding stories of Christian leaders in the main part of the book. Follow the suggestions for determining the next few steps and commit to doing this for at least ninety days. Once you're at least ninety days out and feel you're in a better (not perfect) place of personal application and growth, you'll be more able to serve as a guide for other men on the path.

Mentoring other men can be done one on one or in a group setting. Lots of environments would be appropriate for using this material to lead other men. While this material was specifically designed with the Christian leader in mind, certainly the topic of sexual integrity is appropriate for *any* Christian man. In actuality, every man is in some way a leader, whether with his church, workplace, family or community. In that sense, this book has lots of flexibility. It's just as applicable for use in a small group of pastors as it would be in a very large general men's ministry setting.

Here are only a few of the different formats to consider:

- *One on one:* this could be as a component of an existing mentoring or discipleship relationship or one in which the relationship is defined by walking together for a season to simply address the topic of sexual integrity. This method allows for the most privacy and greatest personal application of content.

- *Small group:* ideally, the group would be two to eight men, which allows for greater personalization and maximum sharing among participants. Again, this could be a component study for an existing group or could be the main purpose for the group for a season of time.

- *Large group:* if this material is being applied in a larger setting of men, there will need to be provision for breaking up the large group into smaller groups to facilitate private sharing and discussion, ideally between two to eight men each.

Of course, one-on-one mentoring will yield a more individualized application of the material and allow for the most privacy. When led well, however, groups have the ability to form lasting relationships among men. They also can allow each participant to learn from one another—including the validation they aren't alone in their contention for sexual integrity. Such groups can offer real opportunity for life-on-life sharpening of each other's integrity and biblical masculinity.

LOOKING TO MENTOR A GROUP

Two words about leading a mentoring group. First, don't expect the individual or group to go any deeper than you're willing to go yourself in the group. If you're not willing to give honest disclosure about your own struggles with sexual integrity, you can't expect those you lead to go any deeper. This is where it's important to do our own work. We can only effectively lead where we're willing to go ahead of them to show them the way.

Second, consider the wisdom for groups just forming to begin with other topics to first build the relationships among the participants. It's not likely that talking about sexual integrity will be the very first conversation they're going to have with each other. To avoid surface-level, abstract conversation around this topic, find a way to allow men in the group to break the ice, hear each other's overall God stories and have some experience swimming together in a lake before heading out to the rip currents off the Atlantic.

LOOKING FOR A MENTOR

If you're looking for a mentor, keep looking and keep praying! Ask older men you trust for suggestions. Watch the life of a possible mentor and observe how he handles everything from his wife and kids to those he leads in ministry. Does he appear to be the same person in a crowd as when he's with one or two people? Does he speak with humility about his own imperfections, whether or not you know the exact nature of those imperfections? Is he respectful of others, especially those with whom he may publicly disagree morally or theologically? Has he gone through his own seasons of pain in his Christian walk without carrying signs of residual bitterness and resentment? These are indicators of a man who's been matured by God.

For such a man, it's worth the risk of asking him to lunch or coffee to share your idea for a mentoring relationship. Even if he says he can't, he'll be gracious in his response and may even help find someone who can. Either way, he will respect what you're doing and be on your side. That's no small thing.

FREE DOWNLOADABLE STUDY GUIDE

I've created a study guide suitable for personal use or for use in leading other men in a mentoring relationship. There's no cost for the study guide for those who sign up for my weekly blog updates, which cover topics such as sexual integrity, Christian leadership and application of Christian principles derived from my work with Christian men as well as my own journey. To get your free copy, go to michaeltoddwilson.com.

Appendix C

ADDITIONAL RESOURCES

■■✝■■

As explained in chapter nine, everyone benefits from healthy relationships with close friends, our wives and our mentors. But for those who need support from more specialized relationships—whether for a season or longer—it can sometimes be overwhelming to know where to turn or who to trust. While not extensive, the following list is intended to help.

SPIRITUAL DIRECTION

The Dallas Willard Center (dallaswillardcenter.com). Spiritual direction center based at Westmont College.

The Transforming Center (transformingcenter.org). Spiritual direction specifically for Christian leaders.

PROFESSIONAL COUNSELOR/COACH

In the United States, professional counselors are licensed at the state level. Each state maintains a list of counselors licensed to practice in that particular state. Certified coaches, however, most often practice in the virtual space of phone and internet connections and do their work independent of geographical restriction. They are designated by certifications such as Board Certified Coach (cce-global.org/bcc) or Master/Professional Certified Coach (coachfederation.org). Additionally, the following resources may be helpful.

American Association of Christian Counselors (aacc.net/resources/find
-a-counselor). General online listing of Christian counselors. This list
is not vetted. Those listed are simply members of the organization.
Also, if you're looking specifically for help with sexual integrity recovery, ask about their qualifications and experience in providing
such specialized services.

Focus on the Family (focusonthefamily.com/counseling/find-a-counselor
.aspx). Provides direct referrals for counseling/coaching consistent
with the organization's values and mission.

Michael Todd Wilson, LPC, BCC (michaeltoddwilson.com). Specialized
professional coaching for men's sexual integrity by phone and video
conference.

MINISTRY TO MINISTERS

CareGivers Forum (caregiversforum.org). A membership organization
that maintains a list of ministries that care for the various needs of
Christian leaders.

Focus on the Family (thrivingpastor.com/caregiving-ministries). Maintains a comprehensive practical helps directory for those in ministry.

INTENSIVE/RESIDENTIAL TREATMENT PROGRAMS

Bethesda Workshops (bethesdaworkshops.org). Extended weekend
residential recovery for sexual addiction in Nashville, Tennessee.

Gateway to Freedom (gatewaymen.com). Extended weekend residential
recovery for sexual addiction in various locations around the country.

Marble Retreat (marbleretreat.org). Residential retreat in Marble,
Colorado, for individuals/couples desiring intensive counseling in
a small group environment with up to three other couples.

Men of Valor (faithfulandtrue.com). Extended weekend residential
recovery for sexual addiction near Minneapolis.

TREK (hopequestgroup.org/trek). Atlanta-area twelve-week residential
recovery program for various forms of addiction, including sexual
addiction. This program meets the requirements of the American

Society of Addictive Medicine (ASAM) for those needing a Level III.5 treatment option and is licensed by the State of Georgia.

SPECIALIZED SUPPORT GROUPS

Celebrate Recovery (celebraterecovery.com). Worldwide, Christ-centered recovery groups for "hurts, hang-ups and habits."

Sexaholics Anonymous (sa.org). Secular Twelve-Step recovery groups specifically for sexual addiction.

Walking Free (hopequestgroup.org/walking-free). Christ-centered recovery group specifically designed for men desiring recovery from sexual brokenness. Based in the Atlanta area, with intentions for replication anywhere willing partnerships can be found.

READING LIST

The following list represents a collection of books I often use in my coaching related to sexual integrity. It's by no means comprehensive. I've included brief descriptions to help you decide which titles might be of interest for your particular situation. Key books in each category are marked with an asterisk (*).

Sexual Addiction and Pursuing Sexual Integrity

Arterburn, Stephen, and Debbie L. Cherry. *Feeding Your Appetites: Take Control of What's Controlling You.* Nashville, TN: Integrity Publishers, 2004. Explores the emotional appetites underlying compulsive and addictive behaviors.

Brown, Michael L. *Can You Be Gay and Christian?* Lake Mary, FL: FrontLine, 2014. Speaks into the gay Christian debate from a solid, biblical-historical perspective.

Carder, David. *Close Calls: What Adulterers Want You to Know About Protecting Your Marriage.* Chicago: Northfield Pub., 2008. Helps identify risk factors for marital affairs from those who've been there.

*Carder, David, and Duncan Jaenicke. *Torn Asunder: Recovering from an Extramarital Affair.* 3rd ed. Chicago: Moody Publishers, 2008. Along with companion workbooks for each spouse, this is a helpful, practical book for couples working toward post-affair healing and reconciliation.

*Carnes, Patrick. *Facing the Shadow: Starting Sexual and Relationship Recovery; A Gentle Path to Beginning Recovery from Sex Addiction.* 2nd ed. Wickenburg, AZ: Gentle Path, 2010. The seminal secular workbook for those desiring to break through denial and take the initial steps in dealing with sexual addiction.

———. *A Gentle Path Through the Twelve Steps: The Classic Guide for All People in the Process of Recovery.* Rev. ed. Center City, MN: Hazelden, 1993. A secular workbook that's exactly what it says it is. Not specifically about sexual integrity, but applicable to recovery from any substance or behavior.

*———. *Recovery Zone: Volume 1.* Carefree, AZ: Gentle Path Press, 2009. Addresses recovery tasks beyond his initial workbook, *Facing the Shadow*.

*Comiskey, Andrew. *Pursuing Sexual Wholeness: How Jesus Heals the Homosexual.* Lake Mary, FL: Creation House, 1989. One of the early books helping Christians who experience same-sex attractions understand how the grace of the cross applies to their lives.

*———. *Strength in Weakness: Overcoming Sexual and Relational Brokenness.* Downers Grove, IL: InterVarsity Press, 2003. A follow-up work to *Pursuing Sexual Wholeness*, this book takes a similar perspective about the cross but applies it to anyone struggling with the larger category of relational brokenness.

*Cusick, Michael John. *Surfing for God: Discovering the Divine Desire Beneath Sexual Struggle.* Nashville, TN: Thomas Nelson, 2012. Personal testimony about escaping the pornography trap, primarily focused on Internet pornography.

*Dallas, Joe. *Desires in Conflict.* Eugene, OR: Harvest House Publishers, 1991. A good general book for understanding the underlying desires in conflict in Christians struggling with same-sex attractions.

*———. *The Game Plan.* Nashville, TN: W Pub. Group, 2005. A simple but effective thirty-day devotional exercise for men desiring greater sexual integrity, with alternating reading and journaling exercises.

*Daugherty, Jonathan. *Grace-Based Recovery*. Raleigh, NC: Lulu.com, 2013. Helpful biblical perspective on the grace so often missing in many recovery programs, even Christian ones.

*Hart, Archibald D. *Thrilled to Death: How the Endless Pursuit of Pleasure Is Leaving Us Numb*. Nashville, TN: Thomas Nelson, 2007. Explores the compulsive aspect underlying all addictions.

Hill, Wesley. *Washed and Waiting: Reflections on Christian Faithfulness and Homosexuality*. Grand Rapids: Zondervan, 2010. Personal testimony from an evangelical Christian single adult who experiences exclusive same-sex attractions.[1]

Laaser, Mark R. *Becoming a Man of Valor*. Kansas City, MO: Beacon Hill Press of Kansas City, 2011. Addresses three big-picture questions from the New Testament for those pursuing greater integrity.

*———. *Healing the Wounds of Sexual Addiction*. Grand Rapids: Zondervan, 2004. An overall good text for understanding sexual addiction from a Twelve-Step perspective.

*———. *Taking Every Thought Captive*. Kansas City, MO: Beacon Hill Press of Kansas City, 2011. Focuses on the mental perspectives necessary to practically apply Scripture's admonition on taking our thoughts captive.

*Larkin, Nate. *Samson and the Pirate Monks: Calling Men to Authentic Brotherhood*. Nashville, TN: W Pub. Group, 2007. Part autobiography and part model for establishing a type of radically transparent men's support community, this book not only tells the story of sexual addiction but also establishes a template for highly relational men's ministry that supports a variety of common struggles among men.

Maltz, Wendy, and Larry Maltz. *The Porn Trap: The Essential Guide to Overcoming Problems Caused by Pornography*. New York: Collins, 2008. A secular book serving as a comprehensive introduction to starting sexual integrity recovery.

*Moberly, Elizabeth R. *Homosexuality: A New Christian Ethic*. Cambridge: James Clarke, 1983. Explores an underlying theme beneath the surface for some who experience same-sex attractions.

Sex Addicts Anonymous. Houston: International Service Organization
of SAA, Inc., 2005. The primary secular text of Sex Addicts Anonymous, containing teaching and stories from those going through
SAA Twelve-Step recovery for sexual addiction.

Sexaholics Anonymous. New and rev. ed. Simi Valley, CA: SA Liter-
ature, 1989. The primary secular text of Sexaholics Anonymous, the
"white" book contains teaching and stories from those going
through SA Twelve-Step recovery for sexual addiction.

*Struthers, William M. *Wired for Intimacy: How Pornography Hijacks
the Male Brain.* Downers Grove, IL: InterVarsity Press, 2009. An
excellent resource discussing the dangerous impact of pornography
on the male brain.

*Tripp, Paul David. *Whiter Than Snow: Meditations on Sin and Mercy.*
Wheaton, IL: Crossway Books, 2008. Devotional based on David's confessions in Psalm 51, with a creative balance between heart and mind.

Willingham, Russell. *Breaking Free: Understanding Sexual Addiction & the
Healing Power of Jesus.* Downers Grove, IL: InterVarsity Press, 1999. A
great discussion about moving into freedom from sexual addiction.

Healthy Sexuality, Marriage, Singleness and Masculinity

*Allender, Dan B. *The Wounded Heart.* Colorado Springs, CO: NavPress,
1990. Along with a companion workbook, this book helps bring emotional and spiritual healing to adults impacted by childhood sexual
abuse.

Crabb, Lawrence J., and Don Hudson. *The Silence of Adam: Becoming
Men of Courage in a World of Chaos.* Grand Rapids: Zondervan,
1995. Addresses the masculine tendency toward passivity and lack
of initiative in all relationships.

Duke, William Marshall. *On the Road: Meditations for Men Who
Travel.* Kansas City, KS: Beacon Hill, 2009. A men's devotional with
specific applications to men's issues, including sexual integrity.

*Eldredge, John. *Wild at Heart: Discovering the Passionate Soul of a
Man.* Nashville, TN: Thomas Nelson, 2001. A popular and refreshing
men's book on the three basic desires underlying the masculine heart.

*Hart, Archibald D., and Sharon May. *Safe Haven Marriage: Building a Relationship You Want to Come Home To.* Nashville, TN: W Publishing Group, 2003. Explores the underlying needs each partner brings into marriage, from the perspective of attachment theory.

*Laaser, Debra. *Shattered Vows: Hope and Healing for Women Who Have Been Sexually Betrayed.* Grand Rapids: Zondervan, 2008. Written by the wife of Mark Laaser, this book shares from a wife's perspective the impact of her husband's addiction on her and on their marriage.

*Laaser, Mark R., and Debra Laaser. *Seven Desires: Looking Past What Separates Us to Learn What Connects Us.* Reprint ed. Grand Rapids: Zondervan, 2013. Explores the seven underlying desires we all have as people, especially applied to Christian marriage.

*McCluskey, Christopher, and Rachel McCluskey. *When Two Become One: Enhancing Sexual Intimacy in Marriage.* Grand Rapids: F. H. Revell, 2004. A male-friendly text for promoting biblical perspectives on marital sexuality.

*Medinger, Alan P. *Growth into Manhood: Resuming the Journey.* Colorado Springs, CO: Waterbrook Press, 2000. A practical book for Christians experiencing same-sex attractions who feel that stunted emotional development in their growing up years is a core part of their story.

Payne, Leanne. *Crisis in Masculinity.* Westchester, IL: Crossway Books, 1985. A classic work exploring the crises in masculinity since the sexual revolution.

Penner, Clifford, and Joyce Penner. *Restoring the Pleasure.* Dallas, TX: Word Pub., 1993. A practical behavioral training manual either for couples working toward initial consummation of marriage or couples re-entering sexual relationship with each other after a season apart.

*Penner, Clifford, and Joyce Penner. *The Way to Love Your Wife: Creating Greater Love and Passion in the Bedroom.* Carol Stream, IL: Tyndale House Publishers, 2007. Helps men understand a wife's perspective on sexuality, presented in a way men can appreciate.

Piper, John. *What's the Difference? Manhood and Womanhood Defined According to the Bible.* Westchester, IL: Crossway Books, 1990. A much-condensed version of *Recovering Biblical Manhood and Womanhood,* giving biblical basis for gender differences in ways supportive of a historically Christian worldview.

*Rosenau, Douglas. *A Celebration of Sex.* Nashville, TN: Oliver Nelson, 1994. A well-rounded guide for couples desiring to enhance intimacy and lovemaking, complete with practical exercises for the couple.

———. *A Celebration of Sex for Newlyweds.* Nashville, TN: Thomas Nelson, 2002. An excellent, condensed version of his larger work, but specifically tailored for newlyweds.

Rosenau, Douglas, and Deborah Neel. *Total Intimacy: A Guide to Loving by Color.* Atlanta, GA: Sexual Wholeness Resources, 2014. Uses colors to creatively discuss three main areas for meaningful and passionate sex within Christian marriage.

Rosenau, Douglas, and Jim Childerston. *A Celebration of Sex after 50.* Nashville, TN: Thomas Nelson, 2004. A modified version of the main text, with targeted application for couples over fifty.

*Rosenau, Douglas, and Michael Todd Wilson. *Soul Virgins: Redefining Single Sexuality.* Atlanta, GA: Sexual Wholeness Resources, 2012. A comprehensive book supporting a practical theology of single-adult sexuality from a distinctly Christian worldview.

Stedman, Rick. *Your Single Treasure: The Good News About Singles and Sexuality.* Chicago: Moody Press, 2000. A solid biblical perspective on single adulthood.

Spiritual Formation

*Barton, Ruth Haley. *Invitation to Solitude and Silence: Experiencing God's Transforming Presence.* Downers Grove, IL: InterVarsity Press, 2004. Written by a spiritual director of ministers, this is a practical book on these two spiritual disciplines.

*———. *Sacred Rhythms: Arranging Our Lives for Spiritual Transformation.* Downers Grove, IL: InterVarsity Press, 2006. An overall good

read on spiritual formation, with practical exercises for personal application of spiritual disciplines.

*Biehl, Bobb. *Mentoring: How to Find a Mentor and How to Become One*. Lake Mary, FL: Aylen, 2005. A very practical book from a Christian leader who's invested decades to promoting its value.

Caliguire, Mindy. *Spiritual Friendship*. Downers Grove, IL: InterVarsity Press, 2007. An easy primer on pursuing and building spiritual friendships.

Curtis, Brent, and John Eldredge. *The Sacred Romance: Drawing Closer to the Heart of God*. Nashville, TN: Thomas Nelson, 1997. Uncovers the spiritual conflict surrounding God's romantic pursuit of our hearts.

Hendricks, Howard G., and William Hendricks. *As Iron Sharpens Iron: Building Character in a Mentoring Relationship*. Chicago,: Moody Press, 1995. A comprehensive text helping Christian men pursue intentional mentoring relationships.

Hill, Wesley. *Spiritual Friendship*. Grand Rapids: Brazos Press, 2015. A thorough discourse on the importance of friendships among Christians, from the perspective of a man who is quite candid about the difficulties but absolute necessity of such friendships as a never-married celibate man with exclusive same-sex attractions.

Kaam, Adrian L. *Spirituality and the Gentle Life*. Denville, NJ: Dimension Books, 1974. Shares how gentleness is a pathway to unlock our experience of the fruit of the Holy Spirit.

Kendall, R. T. *God Meant It for Good*. Charlotte, NC: Morningstar, 1988. An insightful study into the life of Joseph, illustrating how God accomplishes his purposes through the ups and downs of life.

Manning, Brennan. *The Ragamuffin Gospel*. Sisters, OR: Multnomah, 2000. A classic meditation on grace, from the perspective of a Franciscan priest.

May, Gerald G. *Addiction and Grace: Love and Spirituality in the Healing of Addictions*. San Francisco, CA: HarperOne, 2006. A classic book on addiction from a contemplative spirituality perspective.

Moon, Gary W. *Falling For God: Saying Yes to His Extravagant Proposal.* Colorado Springs, CO: Shaw Books, 2004. A gentle journey inviting us deeper into our relationship with Jesus.

Ortberg, John. *The Life You've Always Wanted: Spiritual Disciplines for Ordinary People.* Grand Rapids: Zondervan, 1997. A down-to-earth primer for commonly practiced spiritual disciplines.

Swenson, Richard A. *Margin: Restoring Emotional, Physical, Financial, and Time Reserves to Overloaded Lives.* Colorado Springs, CO: NavPress, 1992. A book about boundaries, as applied to various areas of life.

*Thomas, Gary. *Authentic Faith: The Power of a Fire-Tested Life; What If Life Isn't Meant to Be Perfect but We Are Meant to Trust the One Who Is?* Grand Rapids: Zondervan, 2002. Modern lessons from Christian classics on how God uses difficulty and suffering to accomplish a deep work in us.

———. *Every Body Matters: Strengthening Your Body to Strengthen Your Soul.* Grand Rapids: Zondervan, 2011. A very practical book about the spiritual formation principles underlying the healthy care of our bodies.

*Wiersbe, Warren W. *The Strategy of Satan: How to Detect and Defeat Him.* Wheaton, IL: Tyndale House, 1979. Discusses four main ways Satan attacks the believer's life, along with related strategies for defeating him.

Wolff, Pierre. *May I Hate God?* New York: Paulist Press, 1979. A controversial little text promoting radical honesty in our relationship with God, even with our less-than-desirable emotions.

Other Related Topics

While these aren't directly related to sexual integrity, I've worked with enough clients who benefited to include them here.

Burns, Bob, Tasha Chapman, and Donald C. Guthrie. *Resilient Ministry: What Pastors Told Us About Surviving and Thriving.* Downers Grove, IL: InterVarsity Press, 2013. Presents learning from a roundtable discussion among Christian leaders on characteristics that most promote resilience in ministry.

Carter, Les, and Frank B. Minirth. *The Choosing to Forgive Workbook.*
    Nashville, TN: Thomas Nelson, 1997. A practical, hands-on journey
    to help understand and resolve common roots of unforgiveness.
*Carter, Les, and Frank B. Minirth. *The Anger Workbook: An Interactive
    Guide to Anger Management.* Updated ed. Nashville, TN: Thomas
    Nelson, 2012. A practical, hands-on journey to help understand and
    resolve common roots of anger.
Chapman, Gary D. *The 5 Love Languages: The Secret to Love That Lasts.*
    Chicago: Northfield Pub., 2010. A simple exploration of the primary
    ways we prefer expressing and receiving love in relationships.
Clinton, Timothy E., and Gary Sibcy. *Why You Do the Things You
    Do: The Secret to Healthy Relationships.* Nashville, TN: Integrity
    Publishers, 2006. A practical application of attachment theory
    to human behavior.
*Cloud, Henry, and John Sims Townsend. *Boundaries: When to Say Yes,
    When to Say No to Take Control of Your Life.* Grand Rapids: Zondervan,
    1992. A basic primer from a Christian worldview on setting bound-
    aries for healthy relationships.
———. *Safe People: How to Find Relationships That Are Good for You
    and Avoid Those That Aren't.* Grand Rapids: Zondervan, 1995. Ex-
    plores healthy relationships, both in finding safe people and in being
    a safe person.
*Elkin, Allen. *Stress Management for Dummies.* 2nd edition. Hoboken,
    NJ: John Wiley and Sons, 2013. A secular text with pragmatic advice
    on managing stress.
Hemfelt, Robert, and Frank B. Minirth. *We Are Driven: The Compulsive
    Behaviors America Applauds.* Nashville, TN: Thomas Nelson, 1991.
    Uncovers the underlying drive for accomplishment, with an expla-
    nation for its prevalence.
Jennings, Timothy R. *The God-Shaped Brain: How Changing Your View
    of God Transforms Your Life.* Downers Grove, IL: InterVarsity Press,
    2013. An exploration about how our brain was created for space and
    thoughts about God.
London, H. B., and Neil B. Wiseman. *Pastors at Greater Risk.* Rev. ed.

Ventura, CA: Gospel Light, 2003. A classic work for ministers exploring common risk factors in ministry.

*MacDonald, Gordon. *Rebuilding Your Broken World*. Nashville, TN: Oliver-Nelson Books, 1988. A thoughtful and honest confession of lessons learned through his own recovery journey earlier in pastoral ministry.

McGee, Robert S. *Father Hunger*. Ann Arbor, MI: Vine Books, 1993. Discusses the underlying desire we have for a healthy father figure.

*Sande, Ken. *The Peacemaker: A Biblical Guide to Resolving Personal Conflict*. 3rd ed. Grand Rapids: Baker Books, 2004. A comprehensive guide for Christian conciliation.

Welch, Edward T. *When People Are Big and God Is Small: Overcoming Peer Pressure, Codependency, and the Fear of Man*. Phillipsburg, NJ: P & R, 1997. Explores the consequences of people pleasing and how to put God back in his rightful place.

Willingham, Russell. *Relational Masks: Removing the Barriers That Keep Us Apart*. Downers Grove, IL: InterVarsity Press, 2004. Explores common personality coping styles people use in disordered ways for attempting to get primary needs met.

*Wilson, Michael Todd, and Brad Hoffmann. *Preventing Ministry Failure: A ShepherdCare Guide for Pastors, Ministers and Other Caregivers*. Downers Grove, IL: InterVarsity Press, 2007. A practical workbook for helping ministers sustain long-term effectiveness in ministry, based on empirical data from forced-terminated ministers.

Wright, H. Norman. *Recovering from Losses in Life*. Grand Rapids: Fleming H. Revell, 2006. Practical help in the recovery from grief and loss in life.

NOTES

■■✝■■

CHAPTER ONE: WELCOME TO THE PATH

[1]Mark A. White, "Cybersex Temptation and Use Among Clergy: Prevalence and Path Analysis of the Role of Sexuality Education, Isolation, and Consequences as Vulnerability Factors" (PhD diss., Texas Tech University, 2009), p. 58, http://repositories.tdl.org/ttu-ir/bitstream/handle/2346/45370/White_Mark_Diss.pdf.

[2]*Leadership Journal*, "The Leadership Survey on Pastors and Internet Pornography," January 1, 2001, http://www.ctlibrary.com/le/2001/winter/12.89.html. Approximately 50 percent reported it to have been a struggle by history, with approximately 35 percent reporting it as a current struggle at the time of the survey.

CHAPTER TWO: OUR FELLOW JOURNEYMEN

[1]www.mensfraternity.com.

[2]C. S. Lewis, *The Problem of Pain* in *The Complete C. S. Lewis Signature Classics* (New York: HarperCollins, 2002), p. 604.

CHAPTER THREE: THE MENTAL PATHWAYS OF MEN

[1]Thanks to Rick Stedman, in his book *Your Single Treasure: The Good News about Singles and Sexuality* (Chicago: Moody Press, 2000), p. 88, for encouraging me to research this for myself.

CHAPTER FOUR: THE GRACE-BASED PATH

[1]Michael Todd Wilson and Brad Hoffmann, *Preventing Ministry Failure: A ShepherdCare Guide for Pastors, Ministers and Other Caregivers* (Downers Grove, IL: InterVarsity Press, 2007), p. 16.

CHAPTER FIVE: THE DISCIPLINE OF SURRENDER

[1]These are posted on my website at michaeltoddwilson.com.

[2]Joe Dallas, *The Game Plan* (Eugene, OR: Harvest House Publishers, 1991), p. 58.

[3]SAA, Inc, *Sex Addicts Anonymous* (Houston: International Service Organization of SAA, Inc., 2005).

[4]There is disagreement among Christian circles if masturbation belongs in the red circle. I believe it does for the vast majority of men, due to it being a heart issue more than an external behavior issue. For those interested, I've written more extensively about this in my book *Soul Virgins*. For the present discussion, the reader should place this where he thinks it fits best.

[5]This conceptualization comes from Henry Cloud and John Townsend's classic book, *Boundaries*.

[6]The decision to add a spouse to an Internet monitoring report is a healthy decision for some couples and an unhealthy one for others. This is where feedback from a professional coach or counselor can be helpful.

CHAPTER SIX:
THE DISCIPLINE OF RADICAL HONESTY WITH SELF

[1]Figure 6.1 is adapted from Beverly Hartz, "Pastoral Care and Chaplaincy" class notes, Fall 2000, Talbot Theological Seminary.

[2]More on the importance of safe relationships for Christian leaders is in chapter nine.

[3]Keep in mind, there are many pitfalls to navigate in the realm of full sexual disclosure. This step is best taken with and directed by a therapist or professional coach seasoned in working with men and couples in sexual integrity recovery.

[4]Michael Todd Wilson and Brad Hoffmann, *Preventing Ministry Failure: A ShepherdCare Guide for Pastors and Other Caregivers* (Downers Grove, IL: InterVarsity Press, 2007), pp. 179-82.

CHAPTER SEVEN:
THE DISCIPLINE OF NONMINISTRY GOD TIME

[1]Incidentally, the Greek word for "help" here, *boētheia*, is often applied to the life-saving help of physicians.

[2]Taken from the Serenity Prayer by Reinhold Niebuhr.

CHAPTER EIGHT: THE DISCIPLINE OF BODY MAINTENANCE

[1]Garden-variety depression and anxiety are often well-treated by primary physicians. However, if symptoms are strong enough or unusual enough, these may warrant a psychiatrist from the beginning.

[2]Allen Elkin, *Stress Management for Dummies*, 2nd ed. (Hoboken, NJ: John Wiley and Sons, 2013), pp. 175-84.

[3]"Ten Minutes of Intermittent Movement for Every Hour of Sitting May Counteract Ill Health Effects of Prolonged Sitting," Peak Fitness by Mercola.com, http://fitness.mercola.com/sites/fitness/archive/2014/09/19/intermittent-movement-prolonged-sitting.aspx.

CHAPTER NINE: THE DISCIPLINE OF INTIMATE RELATIONSHIPS

[1]Michael Todd Wilson and Brad Hoffman, *Preventing Ministry Failure: A ShepherdCare Guide for Pastors, Ministers and Other Caregivers* (Downers Grove, IL: InterVarsity Press, 2007), pp. 43-63.

[2]Check out Bobb's website at www.bobbbiehl.com.

[3]Ethically, professional coaches like myself maintain clear boundaries about psychological issues we can't effectively address in coaching. These issues are screened on the front end of any coaching relationship. In this kind of coaching, however, there's necessarily more directed focus on behavioral change and related emotional growth than with other professional coaches. More information about my professional coaching services can be found on my website at michaeltoddwilson.com.

[4]These are the best-case scenarios, which more often happen when a third-party advocate (such as Dr. Don Hicks at churchresourcesolutions.com) helps create a healthy exit strategy that's a "win-win" for both leader and organization. In worst-case scenarios, leaders are terminated immediately without severance or financial support. This may seem to "serve justice" by some terminating organizations. But unintended consequences result not only for the minister, but also for their spouse and children, who often have no financial safety net posttermination.

[5]As of the date of this writing, they even have a few groups exclusively for pastors.

CHAPTER TEN: PURSUING THE PATH OF HOPE

[1]For thoughts on helping mentor other Christian leaders along the path of sexual integrity, see appendix B.

[2]This parable is an accurate representation of real science, by the way. The last few decades of brain research reveal human brains are much more changeable than once thought. Our thinking and behaviors create literal neural pathways in our brains that either grow stronger with reinforcement or atrophy with lack of use. While new thoughts and behaviors may be more difficult to establish initially, they nevertheless create new neural pathways in our brains. What neuroscience only recently discovered was explained two thousand years ago by the apostle Paul when he wrote, "Do not be conformed to this world, but be transformed by the renewal of your mind" (Rom 12:2). One more reason we can trust God's Word.

[3]Dietrich Bonhoeffer, *Life Together: The Classic Exploration of Christian Community*, trans. John W. Doberstein (New York: HarperOne, 2009), p. 96.

[4]Steven Curtis Chapman, "Take Another Step," *The Glorious Unfolding* (Reunion, 2013).

APPENDIX C: ADDITIONAL RESOURCES

[1]While I don't prefer his manner of self-labeling, his candid intellectual and theological perspectives on the subject are quite beneficial.

ABOUT THE AUTHOR

Michael Todd Wilson, LPC, LMHC, BCC, is a licensed professional counselor and board certified coach with Intentional Hearts, offering specialized coaching to Christian men in the recovery and pursuit of sexual integrity. He is also director of ShepherdCare, equipping Christian leaders for health and long-term effectiveness in ministry.

This book represents the intersection of two of Michael Todd's (MT's) passionate callings: leading Christian men away from sexual sin and toward a life consistent with their deeper identity in Christ, and supporting Christian ministry leaders toward sustained effectiveness and impact.

For nearly fifteen years, MT worked as a clinician in a traditional counseling practice, serving clients in the greater Orlando and Atlanta areas. His primary focus was working with Christian men and ministry leaders on a variety of men's issues, the most significant of which was sexual integrity. Now MT has taken what he's learned as a professionally trained and board certified coach and made it accessible from anywhere by phone and video conference. Services are available, nationally and internationally.

If you're looking for renewed purpose and freedom—including freedom from sexual addiction—or you simply want to pursue a greater experience of sexual integrity, all it takes is a willingness to risk trusting that the Lord wants to do a work in your life; not to simply set you free from what limits you, but to set you free to more passionately pursue the Lord's calling.

To find out more about MT's professional services, public speaking and other writings, or to schedule a complimentary consultation, call (770) 623-3331 or visit michaeltoddwilson.com.

Leading Christian men and leaders to live
intentionally from their true hearts.

ALSO BY MICHAEL TODD WILSON

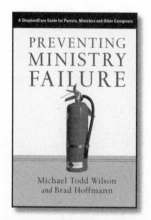

Preventing Ministry Failure
978-0-8308-3444-0